Dor Guez

40 Days

Head of Programming Rachael Hornsby
Gallerist Angelina Radakovic
Marketing and Press Danielle Lucas
Images courtesy of the artist, Dvir Gallery Tel Aviv and
Carlier Gebauer Gallery, Berlin
Design Hyperkit
Translations to Arabic Luay Abdelilah and Omar Al-Qattan
Arabic proofreader Abdel Rahman Abu Shammaleh
English proofreader Suzanne Maguire

This catalogue is published on the occasion of the
exhibition *Dor Guez—40 Days* at The Mosaic Rooms,
London, 12 April—31 May 2013
www.mosaicrooms.org

Supported by A.M. Qattan Foundation

ISBN 978-9950-313-42-2

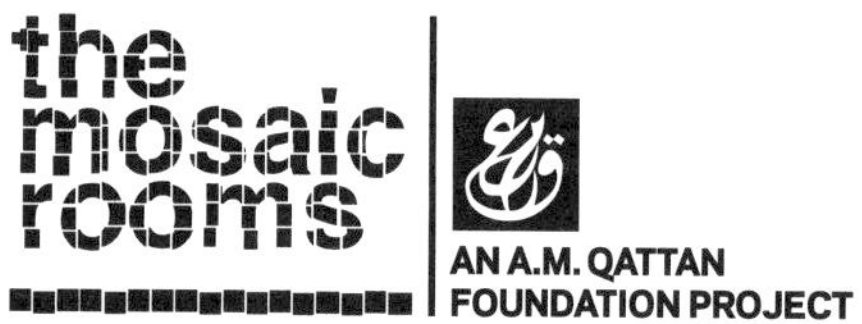

Contents

Disappearing cities of the Arab World— A cultural programme reflecting on the destruction of urban life in the Arab World

Disappearing cities is an ambitious cultural programme of exhibitions, talks and screenings focused on the destruction of Arab urban life in the post-colonial age.

The city is the space where civic life becomes possible; where the tribal, ethnic or confessional divisions of the peoples who settle in it can potentially dissolve and mutate into unfamiliar forms of social order governed by new rules and customs. The city is also a centre of resistance to the invader and of rebellion against injustice. In it also, lovers will meet anonymously, discovering new spaces in the imagination that would have been unthinkable in the countryside or desert, and developing new kinds of relationships. The city transforms our perceptions of childhood; our experiences of light and sound, of space and perspective.

But cities are also great betrayers of their own inhabitants, repositories of vermin and dirt and pollution, as well as theatres of chaos, civil war and massacre. In the modern Arab world, cities have often been profoundly deceitful—promising lawfulness, peace, equality and freedom only to turn into prisons and traps for the unsuspecting citizen, who is often chased out from them or persecuted for the language he speaks or the God she worships (or indeed the one he repudiates).

Jaffa, Beirut, Lydd, Baghdad, Cairo, Aleppo, Basra, Tripoli (Libya *and* Lebanon), Kuwait City, Jerusalem, Mogadishu—these cities have, to varying degrees of course, undergone terrible destruction and violence in the post-colonial age, bearing witness to what can only be described as a failure of the civic project.

Our programme aims to explore the histories and consequences of this failure through art, architecture, literature, music and cinema. Far from a merely academic or nostalgic reflection on the processes that have led to this failure, we plan also to examine how the inhabitants of these cities have continued to resist the breakdown or destruction of their environments through civic projects or artistic expression—or simply through a lovers' union.

This is an ambitious and long-term programme which will initially be structured around a number of events over a one-year period at the Mosaic Rooms in London beginning in Spring 2013 with Dor Guez's show *40 Days*. We also aim to tour some of its outputs to other spaces around the region and internationally. The programme will also be documented in a range of different publications.

The Mosaic Rooms are grateful to Ariella Azoulay for her help in making this show possible, as well as Heidi Zuckerman Jacobson, Director of Aspen Art Museum, who chose Dor Guez to be the International Artist in Residence in ArtPace, San Antonio and to ArtPace, San Antonio for co-producing the *40 Days* project.

Introduction
Omar Al-Qattan

"Beware of saying to them that sometimes different cities
follow one another on the same site and under the same
name, born and dying without knowing one another, without
communication among themselves. At times even the names of
the inhabitants remain the same, and their voices' accent, and
also the features of their faces; but the gods who live beneath
names and above places have gone off without a word and
outsiders have settled in their place."
Italo Calvino, Invisible Cities, 1972, pp30–31

It is a tragic and terrible shame that Dor Guez's first
solo show in London should be held at The Mosaic
Rooms under the shadow of continuing civil war and
confessional violence in the Arab world. We who had
the privilege of growing up in the mixed cities of that
region—Beirut, Damascus, Baghdad, Cairo—have
seen those rich urban tapestries break apart. It is as
if the fabric of our region, however rich, ancient and
colourful, simply could not withstand the onslaught
of modernity, whether it took the form of Zionism
and its ethno-colonial project, or secular Arab
nationalism in all its many guises, or, more recently,
Islamic nationalism, in all its varieties. Today, the
bleeding continues—Iraq has lost many of its most
ancient minorities, Syria will probably go the same
way, Lebanon is an ethnic and confessional time
bomb, Israel's Palestinian citizens and those living
under occupation are increasingly marginalised and
threatened with expulsion, and Egypt's Copts are
living in profound insecurity. Needless to say, citizens
of all ethnicities and confessions, particularly the poor
and disenfranchised, also find themselves hostage to
unspeakable injustice and destruction—a condition
tragically shared with many other regions in the
world today.

However, this reality was also one of the reasons
we chose to invite Dor Guez to show at The Mosaic
Rooms. For Guez is a product of a rare mixity that

was ironically the result of two major, but antithetical historical events: the expulsion of most of Palestine's citizens from their homeland in 1948, and the subsequent creation of the state of Israel, of which he is now a citizen. Guez's mother is from Al-Lydd[1], daughter of one of the few Palestinian families to remain in the city after most of its 20,000 inhabitants were driven out and never allowed to return after the 1948 war. Guez's heritage is also Tunisian Jewish on his father's side, immigrants to the new state of Israel in 1950s and to Al-Lydd, subsequently renamed Lod. It is no surprise then that his work should be so preoccupied with the dynamics of majority-minority relations, with the disappearance of minority cultures, and with the personal—yet often heroic—attempts to keep their memories alive. But this work also invites us to question our own definitions of nationalism and ethnicity and to reflect on the writing of history, as the artist explains later in this book, in his conversation with Mitra Abbaspour.

As a child growing up in Beirut in the 1970s, I was discouraged from enquiring about a person's religion, even though it was extremely difficult to miss the undercurrents of confessional divisions all around us (or indeed the ostentatious religious symbols worn by many people). My parents, like many secular nationalists of the time, dreamt of a society free from these divisions and kept referring to a past—but which past?—in which everyone lived in harmony, Muslims, Christians and Jews (rarely were atheists mentioned in that context). It was in that spirit that we were ordered not to discriminate between people on the basis of their religion. Yet perhaps our parents were also idealistic and naïve, for they underestimated the depth of confessional loyalties and the extent to which our societies remained entangled in the Ottoman system of majority rule and minority autonomy, which clearly could no longer function in the post-war realities of the Levant.

In that sense, as we hope you will see from this rich and moving exhibition, Guez's work is also a reaffirmation of different possibilities for his city and, by extension, for the region. He offers a defiant assertion of a continuing *presence* in the face of historical erasure and a seemingly relentless contemporary dynamic of denial and destruction that is both violent and irrational. This artistic assertiveness, archival and fragile as it is, and shrouded in tragedy, nonetheless uncovers something else: an obstinate, clinging presence that will not go away. *40 Days*, as Guez's show is entitled, marks the end of the period of mourning, the cusp, as it were, between remembering and starting anew. A Christian Palestinian *archive*[2] for sure, but one brought to forceful life by a *living* descendant, even if his identity has been reshaped by history and circumstance. But then which one of us can claim an unchanging identity?

My own paternal grandmother was born in Al-Lydd and the city was the last place of refuge for my father's family as they fled Palestine in Summer 1948, on their long way to exile in Amman, Jordan. So it is particularly fitting—and ironic—that Guez's show should today be hosted here in London: two descendants of Lyddites, one Israeli Palestinian and the other British Palestinian, reaffirming a common past in the capital city of the old empire, which holds so much of the responsibility for the collapse of an ancient, tolerant and open Levant and, tragically, whose more recent meddling in the region has proven equally catastrophic.

London, Spring 2013

Omar Al-Qattan is a filmmaker and a Trustee of the A.M. Qattan Foundation. He currently directs The Mosaic Rooms' artistic programme.

---

1 The city is famous as the birthplace of St George's mother. He is revered by all the monotheistic religions in Palestine as a saint (under different names, including al-khader) and also patron saint of England. Yet its Arab Christian and Muslim histories are hardly visible today and it has become notorious as the drugs ghetto of Israel and one of its poorest and most violent urban centres.

2 See pp11 for further details about this archive

Photographs, like a sort of embodied, physical subconscious
Mitra Abbaspour in conversation with Dor Guez

Mitra Abbaspour: Let's begin at the beginning. When and in what context did you begin working with historic photographs?

Dor Guez: I started working with archives in 2006, as a part of my studies and my PhD research on Orientalist style photography in the Zionist archives. Three years later I started working with archival footage as a visual artist and not only as a writer.

In 2009, I found a suitcase under my grandparents' bed, packed with plastic bags filled with photographs and other documents from the first half of the 20th century. I had never seen these materials before, and I remember wondering why they were not organised in family albums as is the habit with these sorts of photographs (weddings, baptisms, studio photographs for Christmas, etc). With my grandparents' permission, I took on the task of organising them into albums. I tried to build the conventional narratives of family albums and to organise them accordingly. As the unofficial historian of the family, and maybe also as the eldest grandson, my grandparents let me deal with these materials. I found myself editing our histories over and over again in various versions and possibilities, but I failed with the primary task of making family albums. I realised what my grandmother understood all along: it is an impossible mission. She gave me time to reach that conclusion on my own, and to fail on my own, as she had in the past.

MA: What is the significance of working with this historic material for your work?

DG: This accidental encounter with a single suitcase was the starting point of the Christian Palestinian Archive (CPA) project, which is the only archive today dedicated to the Christian Palestinian diaspora. The CPA was also a turning point in my

artistic practice, and it provides the basis for all of my installations:
it can be one picture, or a series of 15 photographs dressed as a
family album. It was when I started writing, recording and filming
(as a part of my attempt to contextualise the materials) that I
realised why my grandmother had packed them compactly and
put them away under my grandfather's side of the bed, like a sort
of embodied, physical subconscious. One cannot classify them in
the common genre of "family albums"; they are evidence of a life
"before" and "after" (some of them even "during") one year (1948)
and an ongoing catastrophe.

**MA: The material qualities of the original photograph—its
surface texture, tears and creases, and evidence of handling—
are high-lighted in what you call a "scanogram". What is the
importance of emphasising that the historic photograph is not
only an image, but also an object?**

DG: You described it correctly. The meaning of the term
"scanogram" is literally drawing with a scanner machine. Every
scanogram is made by three layers of scanning, each scan is
programmed to feature a different aspect of the material, and then
I compose the layers into one image. A scanogram is my personal
interpretation of historical material from the CPA. Naturally, the
process relies on a personal perspective and the outcome differs
from the original photograph. This technique of multi-scanning
stresses the history of the document as an object, meaning the
rips and tears become very prominent in an almost abstracted
way and take on a three-dimensional format in their size and scale.
The scanograms offer ways of re-presenting these documents and
seeing them through sharp, high resolution prints. Scanograms are
activated as contemporary 'objects' or, to be more accurate, as a
result of their contemporary physical condition.

In other words, the original photograph, as a physical object,
has a history of its own, and the scanograms are trying to bring
this story to the surface.

**MA: As you are describing your process, it strikes me that
once you transform these photographs into scanograms, each
picture effectively has two authors and two dates of creation:
that of its original and then your revival in a new form and
context. How does this historical and authorial dualism reveal
itself in the scanograms?**

DG: Indeed, a scanogram tells two stories (with two dates) that complement each other: the first is in the morphological content of the photograph, "Samira in her wedding gown", for example, and the other is the story of the photograph itself since it was printed: the tears, the folds- the fact that Samira's wedding photographs were saved under the bed and they are not organised and kept "appropriately" in an album. The scanogram of the wedding photograph tells the history of what they refuse to talk about directly. It is exactly the condition of a physical subconscious.

MA: Do you think about your work as an interaction with the original photographer?

DG: Yes, not only by my scanner's interpretation, but also with my act of abandonment of the originals; I almost never keep the original photographs. I scan the photograph or any other document, and send it back. The goal of the CPA is to become an online database, and I have no interest in expropriating the photographs from their original "plastic bags". The materials will probably disappear with time in the hands of their keepers. That is the story of photography; it has a time limit if you don't keep it in archival conditions. I know it is hard to grasp how a person who is dedicated to research in archives can let these original materials go, but this is the nature of this media we call photography, and I respect it. A scanogram, therefore, is only one point in time, one date, which interacts with other dates, when the camera lens snapped and the photograph was printed.

MA: I understand your thoughts, however, I must admit that as a photograph curator, when I was watching *40 Days*, I winced when Samira tore apart the photographs of the Lod cemetery with the sigh, "must be done." At the same time, I was impressed by the symbolic power of this gesture, which emphasises both the physicality and fragility of those photographs as objects and as historical records. What is your relationship to those pictures as evidence and as history? How have those thoughts shaped your artistic practice?

DG: I definitely share your feeling of unease; when it happened, I took a deep breath watching her damaging them so severely. I could have taken the photographs from her hands, and separated them gently from the humidity that pasted them together, but it was her prerogative. Now, it is the story of these images as objects, and in order to tell the full story this act "must be done". The two stories of the photograph intersect here in a poetic way: the morphological content is the documentation of destruction, and the terrible way those photo-graphs were held and then separated, the history of the photograph as an object, is a second layer of destruction.

The *40 Days* video is an opportunity to watch an expedited process of interference in the original photographs. I sat with Samira in the living room, the camera between us, and we talked about the latest destruction of the Christian cemetery in our town. While we were talking about it, she told me that my grandfather, Ya'qoub (Jacob), took photographs to document this violent act for the police, as official evidence. It was the only documentation of the demolition, and since the police didn't solve the case, he got them back. Samira kept them in a kitchen drawer, where they were exposed to moisture from her cooking, and she sent me to find them while we were shooting. Usually, my scanograms reflect years of weathering, but in this case the story of the object was built in minutes, while the camera is filming. This video keeps the same logic of the CPA as an archive based on digital scans. It is her photograph, and it is her right as the owner to destroy it, and to hide it in her kitchen.

MA: *40 Days* opens with statistics about the Christian Palestinian minority of Lod, and of Israel, as well as an account of the repeated vandalism of the town's Christian cemetery. Against a backdrop of these cold facts, a hauntingly intimate portrait of a couple unfolds. The snapshots that Ya'qoub took to document the vandalism of the cemetery and Samira's explanation of them, as if pages from a family album, bridge the political and the personal. When did you learn about these pictures of the cemetery? Did you ever discuss them with Ya'qoub? How do you relate the two halves of this film: the subject of the Lod cemetery and of Ya'qoub and Samira?

DG: Ya'qoub, Samira and I never talked about the pictures before. As the camera is our third eye, all stories started when the camera is operated. It immediately creates a new array of relations between us. As for the two narratives in the video, you put it accurately. Like most of my video works, *40 Days* offers a deeply personal story which relates to a larger narrative. In this case, it is the death of Ya'qoub and his memorial service, 40 days later and, at the

same time, the story of the place where he is buried, the Christian
cemetery in Lod, which every few years is being vandalised by other
religious groups. It is a hate crime. Maybe it is only a question of
time before his grave will be damaged as well. The destruction of
the cemetery reflects the situation of the Christians as a minority
and, more generally, the human condition of being vulnerable.

**MA: The film is situated historically by its dedication to Ya'qoub
Monayer, who lived from 1920–2011, and in the timeframe laid
out by Samira as she discusses the epitaphs of family graves,
specifically her mother who died in 1979 at age 80. From this
perspective the history of the entire 20th century is cast in
the individual lives of the film's subjects. I see this as related
to your scanograms, which take on complex, overshadowed
chapters of history in the form of personal and candid family
pictures. How do the details of these individuals' lives speak to
more universal concerns?**

DG: Being a minority is the constitutive condition of this century.
It is not only being numerically outnumbered, but a question of
different contexts as well; gender, education, economic status, etc.
In fact, at some point in our lives we all experience the feeling of
being a minority, but for some of us this condition is suppressed.
You can look at my work and reduce it to an aesthetic statement
regarding my culture or the history of my region, even the art
of telling a story—all correct. But, I hope it is also about human
solidarity. The term "minority within a minority" becomes a sort of
metaphor in my work; in my eyes we are all Christian Palestinians.
It is also your cemetery that is being repeatedly destroyed.

**MA: Several times the film lingers on something that is
poignantly absent. I am thinking of the scene of the gravestone
with only half a cross, the imprint of the missing half stained
onto the pale stone back; or the 40-day service in the church,
where a piece of white paper obscures the head of the priest;
or the heart wrenching final scene with one pair of feet
stretching out in the early morning light of a bed, ignoring
the ringing phone. What is the role of absence—visually and
conceptually—in *40 Days*?**

DG: The role of absence is to create a gap for you to fill. It also reflects our inability to tell a full story, both visually and conceptually.

I will expand on one absentee, who requires an explanation: the wrinkled piece of white paper showing in the 40-day memorial service in the video. In past installations, I have dealt with the complex relationship between the Christian community and the Orthodox Church. There is a cultural gap between the church leaders, who are in Europe, and the congregation. In my installation *St. George Church* (2009) you see the priest giving a sermon in Greek, a language that is not understood by the parishioners, while an interpreter from the community translates his words into Arabic. The Sunday mass takes three hours because of this act of translation, and obviously there are many situations "lost in translation." In *40 Days* you see the priest reading from a paper that is being held against his face, so he will remember the names of the deceased family. It is the only time in the video that you actually see a human face, and it is being concealed most of the time by the priest's note, leaving his presence as a remote representation of the religious leadership of the Orthodox Church.

MA: Arabic, its daily vernacular use, and its easy mixture with Hebrew into a local dialect, is a thread that weaves through the film starting with the salutations of the phone calls that open the film and throughout in Samira's conversations, as well as in the final "read" liturgy of the priest. What is the importance of Arabic in telling this story, in painting a portrait of the generation of Ya'qoub and Samira?

DG: Three languages play a role in my videos: Arabic, the mother tongue, which is used for the act of remembering; Hebrew, the acquired tongue, which is mainly used to describe events that happen after the war; and Greek, the religious ritual tongue, which we don't understand at all.

MA: The narrative structure of *40 Days* is poetic. Rather than identifying the characters, illustrating their features, and describing the series of events that transpire within the film, you present a sequence of filmic snapshots of tightly framed gestures, details and symbols.

DG: You describe it beautifully. The story is being told by hand gestures.

MA: The complexity of identity—religious, cultural, linguistic, territorial, historical—is a central subject throughout your work. This complexity is often revealed by partial documents or questions without answers. Please discuss the role of the unknown in your practice?

DG: Yes. It is evident in my work that there are more questions than answers, and you actually leave the work questioning yourself. It is a wonderful state of mind to be in—the condition of asking. The answers will be shaped by the individuals themselves. They are pointed at/for you.

Another thought: we are constantly preoccupied with our own identity—maybe it is a reaction to globalisation, and maybe that's how we've always been. Did you notice that since the internet revolution, there are more and more archives being established? Do you think it is partly a reaction of preserving our singularity?

Maybe it is a topic for our next talk.

MA: What motivates your work?

DG: Memory.
Thank you for your questions.

MA: Thank you for your thoughts, Dor, and most of all for your work.

Mitra Abbaspour is an Associate Curator in the Department of Photography at The Museum of Modern Art in New York. At MoMA, she participates in a collaborative research endeavour to study the material and aesthetic development of photography in the early 20th century. Her doctoral research focused on photographic archives and their methods of writing a history of photography in the Middle East.

"This is a photograph of Lod Ghetto"
Dor Guez

Place and date: Lod, 1949
Event: Samira and Ya'qoub Monayer's wedding
Photographer: Unknown

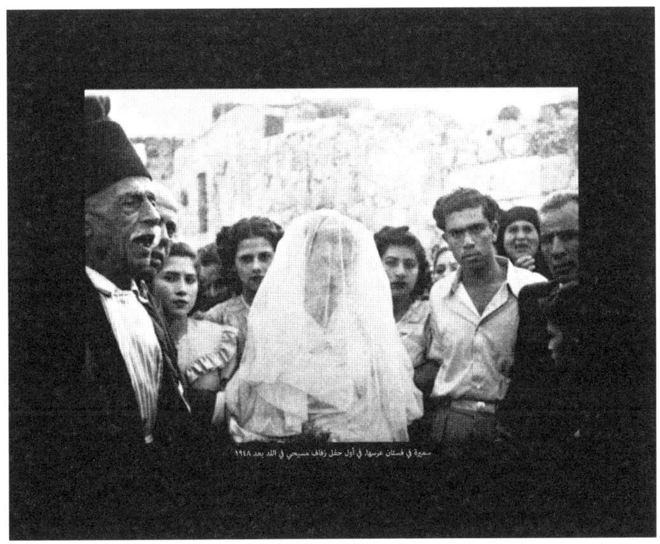

*Scanograms #1, Image 09, Samira
in her wedding gown, the first
Christian wedding in Lod after
1948*, 60 x 75cm, 2010

Two events vie for the role of my very first memory. One is my uncle's
wedding. I was nearly three years old at the time. His bride's fingers
were bedecked with colourful thimbles for the wedding dance. The
blurred flickers of colour generated by the plastic thimbles moving
rhythmically against the white backdrop of her bridal gown are etched
in my mind. I have never asked to see my uncle's wedding album, but
since weddings are usually documented and reported by both citizen
and state, I can probably access the photographic record at will.

The other memory is crisp and more vividly detailed. The
actual event probably occurred around the same time, but it was not
documented, nor can I date it with precision. I do know with certainty
that it took place on a Saturday because that was the day we habitually
went to the beach in the summertime. On that particular, undated

Saturday morning, my grandmother took my brother and me to the beach in Jaffa, the city where she was born in 1932, and where her childhood home was located 100 steps from the Mediterranean. She no longer lived in Jaffa, but that Saturday morning she carried me into the sea, her back serving as my buoy. The water was calm, without waves. My petite grandmother wore a shiny black swimsuit, and I felt as if I were riding on the back of a whale. Flooded by a sense of security mixed with excitement, I glanced back at Jaffa's shore, the town's sand-coloured houses looking tiny on the distant slope.

Several decades later I find myself poring over a photograph of my grandmother's wedding. It was taken by a professional photographer whose name she does not recollect. Her face is shrouded with a translucent chiffon bridal veil, yet one may easily discern her big eyes gazing at the camera. Her painted lips are sealed. Her features resemble those of my mother. She is young and wears a white wedding dress, which separates her from the crowd even as it draws attention to her presence. She is an absent-presence.[1] To her left are her best friend, Nina, and her brother Jack, slimmer and much more handsome than the man I remember from my childhood. She is surrounded by her bridesmaids, dressed in their best, their hair parted and adorned with ribbons, her cousin Rogette to her right, and the groom's sister, Rowaida, behind her.

It is an occasion that is routinely documented: the bride, accompanied by family and friends, leaves her home and goes out into the public domain, inviting city residents to join the celebration. A Muslim woman, identified by her black scarf, is part of the crowd, attesting to the fact that members of other religions were participants in such festivities. Another short woman on the right stretches her neck up high, hoping to be included in the picture. On the left are two men: Tawfik, Samira's uncle, trying to provide the camera with a full view of his face (alas, half remains hidden); and Issa, the groom's uncle, who appears in profile, wearing a Turkish fez and a striped *gallabia* (a traditional Arab garment) with a tailored jacket over it. He doesn't look at the camera. He is on duty, announcing the arrival of the bride, and is captured, mouth wide open, singing in her honour. A certain distance is maintained between the bride and the camera. It is a tacitly observed gap that no one traverses.

I found my grandparents' wedding photographs in 2009 in a white plastic bag inside a frayed suitcase kept under their bed on my grandfather's side. "These are our wedding photos," my grandmother confirmed sixty years after they were taken. "What year was it?" I asked, and she replied, absentmindedly, "a year after 1948," expropriating 1949 from the sequence of time, adjusting to an internal calendar of her own. My grandmother's family was forced to flee Jaffa in 1948, never to return

to their home. This much I knew. And so, I let her be and did not ask
any more questions.

Later that year, while filming the video *July 13*, I heard my grandfather use the term "Lod Ghetto" for the very first time. I was stunned.
In my mind, the term "ghetto" carried different connotations related
to urban slums or to Jewish European history.[2] But my grandfather
repeatedly said, "Lod Ghetto." I googled "Lod Ghetto" and Google
corrected me by asking, "Do you mean Lodz Ghetto?" Later I learned
that the name was given by the military government, established
by Israel after the 1948 war, to a fenced-in area around St. George
Church in Lod. After the city was conquered by the Israeli army in
July 1948, the vast majority of its Palestinian population was forced
to march on foot into exile. Only 1,030 people remained in Lod, and
they were concentrated in a small area surrounded by barbed wire and
placed under military rule and curfews: the Lod Ghetto. The term took
root among the city's old-timers as well as the newly arrived Jewish
immigrants who settled in Lod after 1948, and even today this area of
the city is known as the "ghetto."[3]

In the course of time, photographs blur the images that are etched
in our mind, becoming the official visual representatives of those events.
Undocumented events are often forgotten, carried into the high seas
on one's back. Photography and memory interrelate in diverse ways.
Photographs can compete with, obliterate, reinforce, contradict, affirm,
or otherwise interact with experienced, undocumented recollections. I
have never looked at photographs of my uncle's wedding for fear that the
beauty of my memory would not stand the test of time or taste, that the
photographs would undermine the personal experience. Nevertheless,
it is customary to photograph joyous events, such as weddings, and to
arrange the photographs in an album. The presence of a camera raises
awareness among participants that the event will be recalled and re-
viewed in the future through the resulting images, the most important
of which are often framed and displayed in places of honour.

My grandparents' marriage ceremony was the first Palestinian
wedding held in Lod after 1948. Inadvertently, their wedding photographs have transcended the role of family mementos and become
charged with historical significance as rare archival evidence of life in
Lod Ghetto. After my grandmother hired a photographer, posed for him,
paid for the photographs, and received them, she shoved them all into a
plastic bag, which she buried under the bed. Why didn't she organise the
photographs in an album, as was and still is the custom? The historical
context provides a key to understanding this dissonance. One doesn't
display the pictures of an insult in a family album.

That year I initiated an ongoing project, the Christian Palestinian Archive. It began with the photographs in the series *Scanograms #1*, which refers to the practice of making family albums. The archive as a whole features images traditionally categorised as distinct photographic genres: "passport photographs", "wedding photographs", "class photographs." The documents in the archive did not originate from actual family albums. They were salvaged from scattered plastic bags collected in Lod, Amman, London, Cairo, and Nicosia. Samira Monayer's photograph, shot "a year after 1948", is not from my grandmother's wedding album. Nor is it (just) a photograph of her marriage. It is evidence of her catastrophe.[4] Photographs are often described as capturing decisive moments, but they are also mute. Their silenced meanings emerge in the space between the image and the viewer. The traumatic historical context and the archival display restore this photograph's voice as I write: "This is a photograph of Lod Ghetto."

This article was first published in *Dor Guez—100 Steps to the Mediterranean*, New England Press, 2012

[1] "Present-absentee" is the official term used to designate Palestinians who remained in the country after 1948, but whose land and property were confiscated and handed over to the state. The Absentee Property Law of 1950 grants to the State of Israel the assets of those Palestinians deported from it in the 1948 war. Israel's expulsion of Palestinian civilians in 1948, the confiscation of their property, and the denial of their right to return after the war are actions forbidden by the Geneva Convention (IV) relative to the Protection of Civilian Persons in Time of War. Geneva, August 12, 1949, articles 49 and 53 (see www.icrc.org/ihl.nsf/ FULL/380?OpenDocument, accessed 6/3/12).

[2] The term "ghetto" originated with the Jewish quarter of 16th century Venice, the only area of Venice where Jews were allowed to live. Its name was derived from the foundry (geto in a Venetian dialect) on the site. "Ghetto" has since become the name used for all Jewish quarters throughout Europe. Today the term also denotes a part of a city populated by people of a specific ethnic group or of low socioeconomic status.

[3] Haim Yacobi, The Jewish-Arab City: Spatio-Politics in a Mixed Community (London: Routledge, 2009), 32, 61.

[4] Whereas most of Israel's Jewish citizens refer to the 1948 war as the War of Independence, Palestinians refer to the war and its aftermath as the Nakba, or "Catastrophe". With the establishment of the State of Israel, nearly three-quarters of a million Palestinians were exiled.

Artist's Biography

Dor Guez (b. Jerusalem) is a multi-disciplinary artist whose installations combine diverse modes of video and photographic practices. He is a lecturer in the History and Theory Department at Bezalel Academy of Arts and Design, Jerusalem, and a researcher of archives affiliated with Tel Aviv University. In 2009 he established the first archive devoted to the Christian Palestinian minority of the Middle East.

Guez's solo exhibitions include *Georgiopolis* at the Petach Tikva Museum of Art; *The Monayer Family* at the Jewish Museum, New York; *Al-Lydd* at KW Institute for Contemporary Art, Berlin; *The Nation's Groves* at the Tel Aviv Museum of Art and Carlier Gebauer Gallery, Berlin; *Against The Grain* at Beursschouwburg Art Center, Brussels; *SABIR* at Dvir Gallery, Tel Aviv, *40 Days* at ArtPace, San Antonio, and more. In 2012 the first overview of Guez's work, *100 Steps to the Mediterranean*, was shown at The Rose Art Museum in Boston. His work has also been shown at the 12th Istanbul Biennial; the 17th International Contemporary Art Festival; Videobrasil, São Paulo; the 3rd Moscow International Biennale; Palais de Tokyo, Paris; Benin Biennial; Bucharest Biennial, Tokyo Metropolitan Museum of Photography, and more.

Guez is the recipient of the Orgler Scholarship, Tel Aviv University; Ruth Ann and Nathan Perlmutter Artist in Residency Award, Rose Art Museum, Brandeis University; and International Artist in Residence Award, ArtPace, San Antonio.

40 Days, 'Scanogram', series of manipulated ready-mades,
12 archival inkjet prints, 90 x 65cm /65 x 90cm, 2012

40 يوماً، سكانوغرام، سلسلة من الصور الجاهزة والتي تم التلاعب بها
12 نسخة حبرية أرشيفية ، 65x90 و 90x65 صم 2012

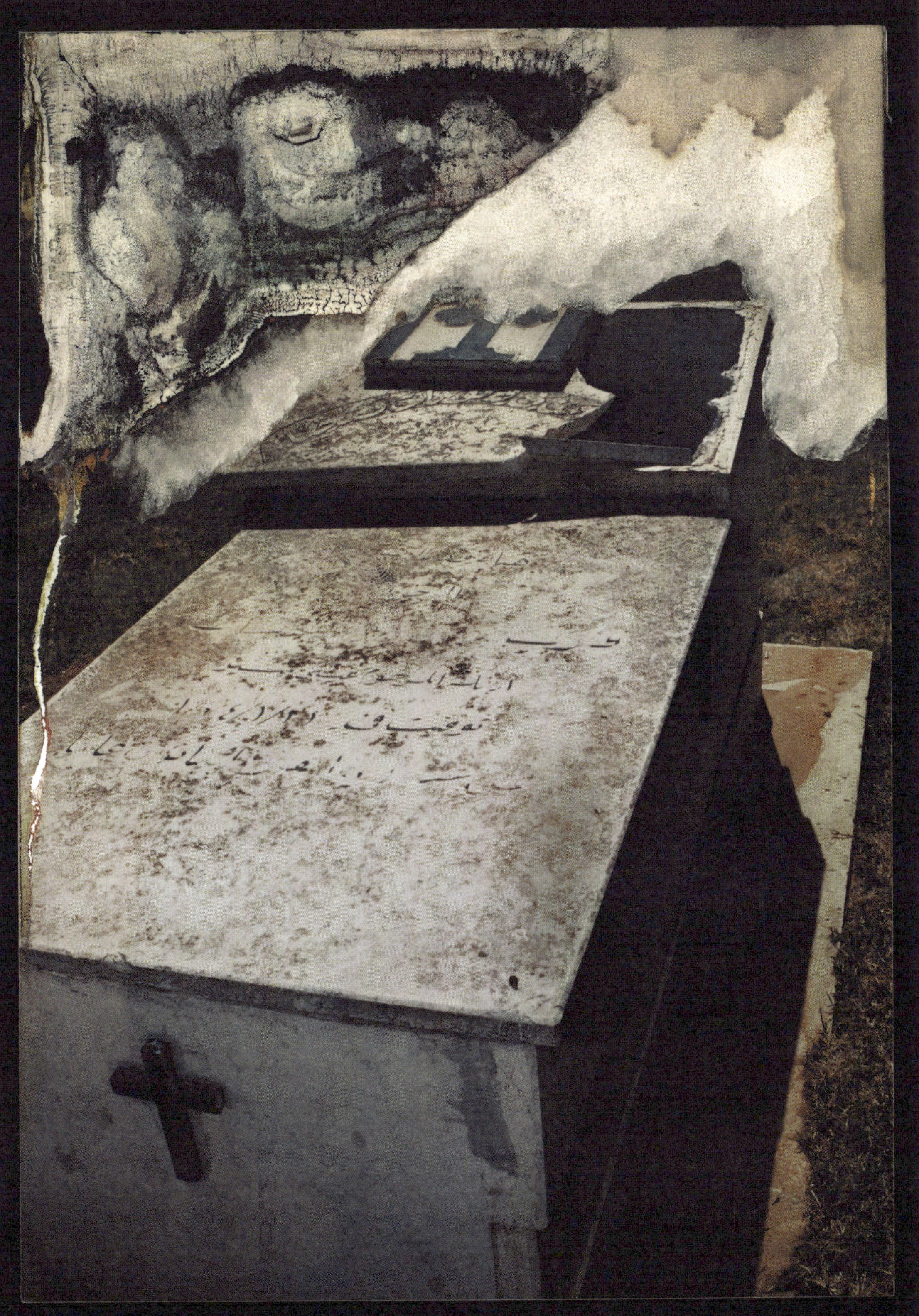

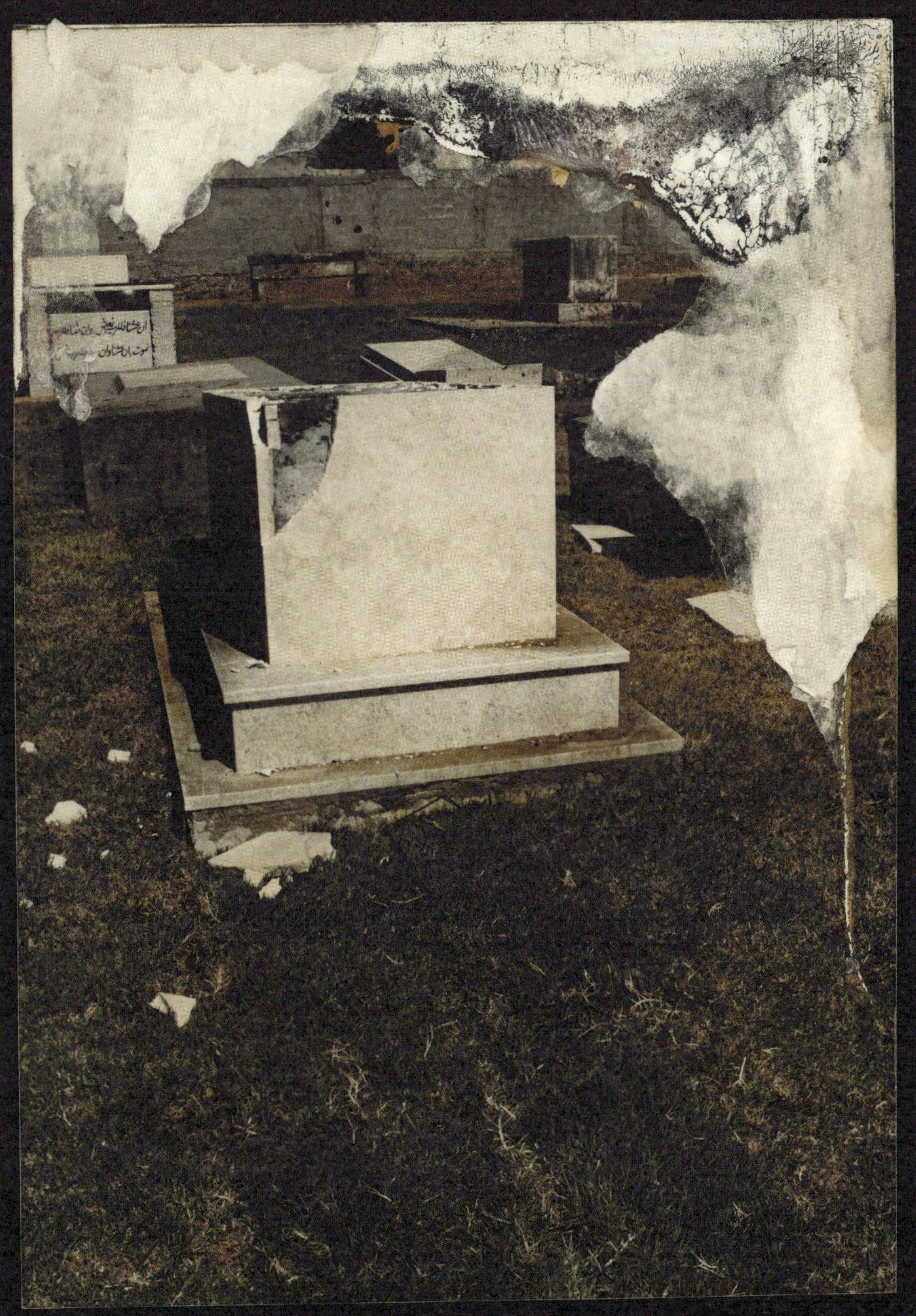

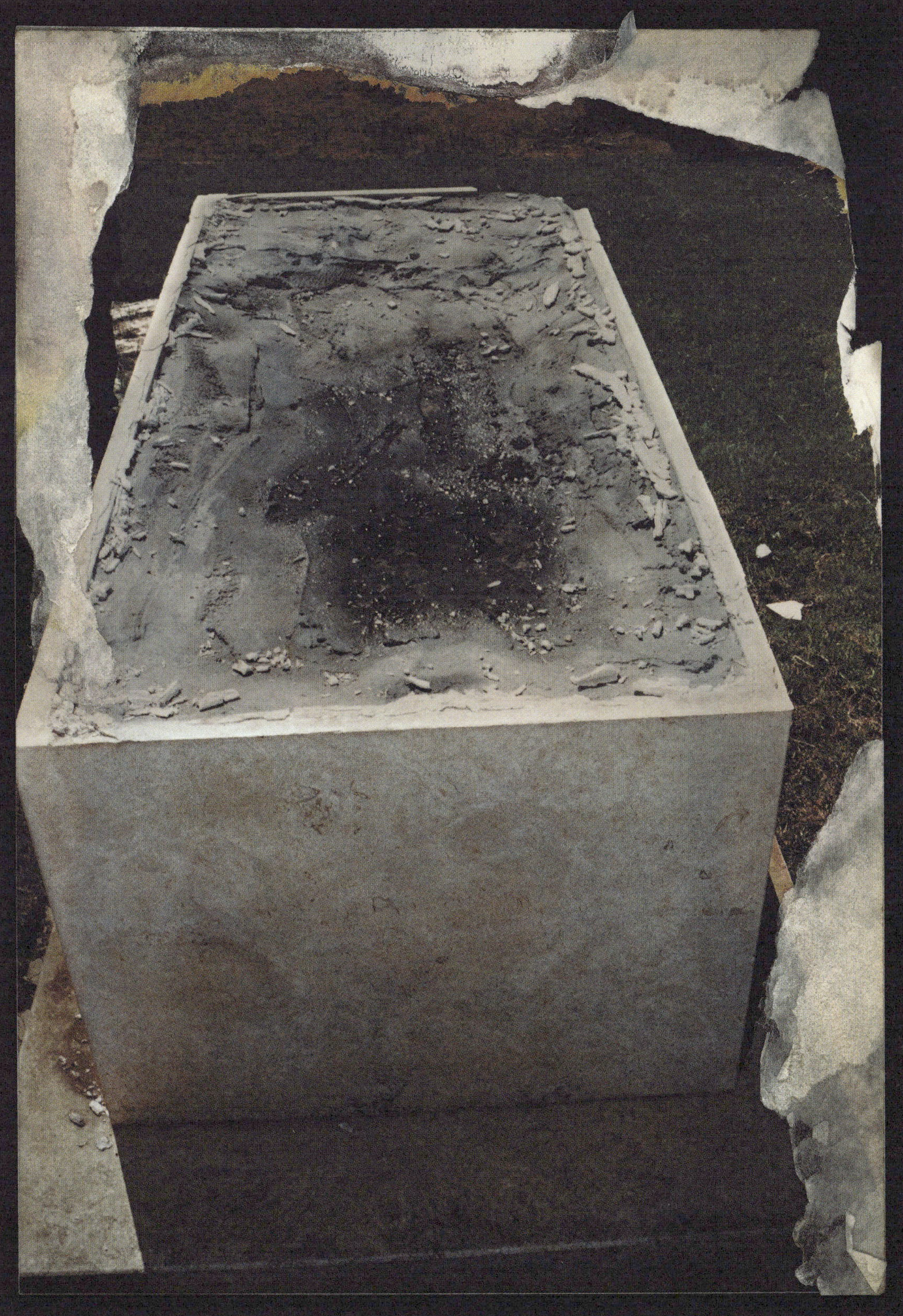

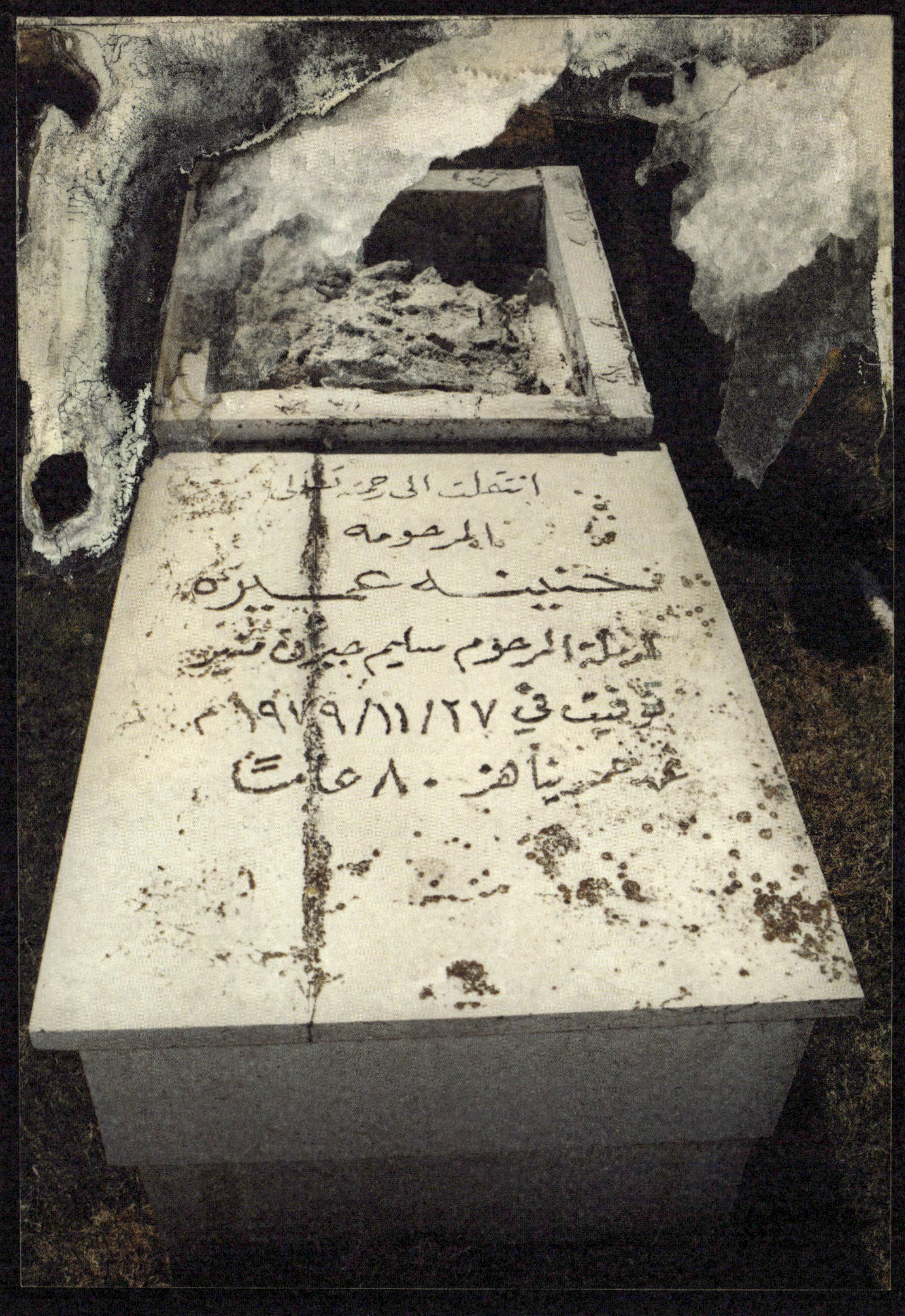
انتقلت الى رحمة الله
المرحومة
فخنينه عميرة
ارملة المرحوم سليم جبران قشوع
توفيت في ١٩٧٩/١١/٢٧
عمرها ٨٠ عاما

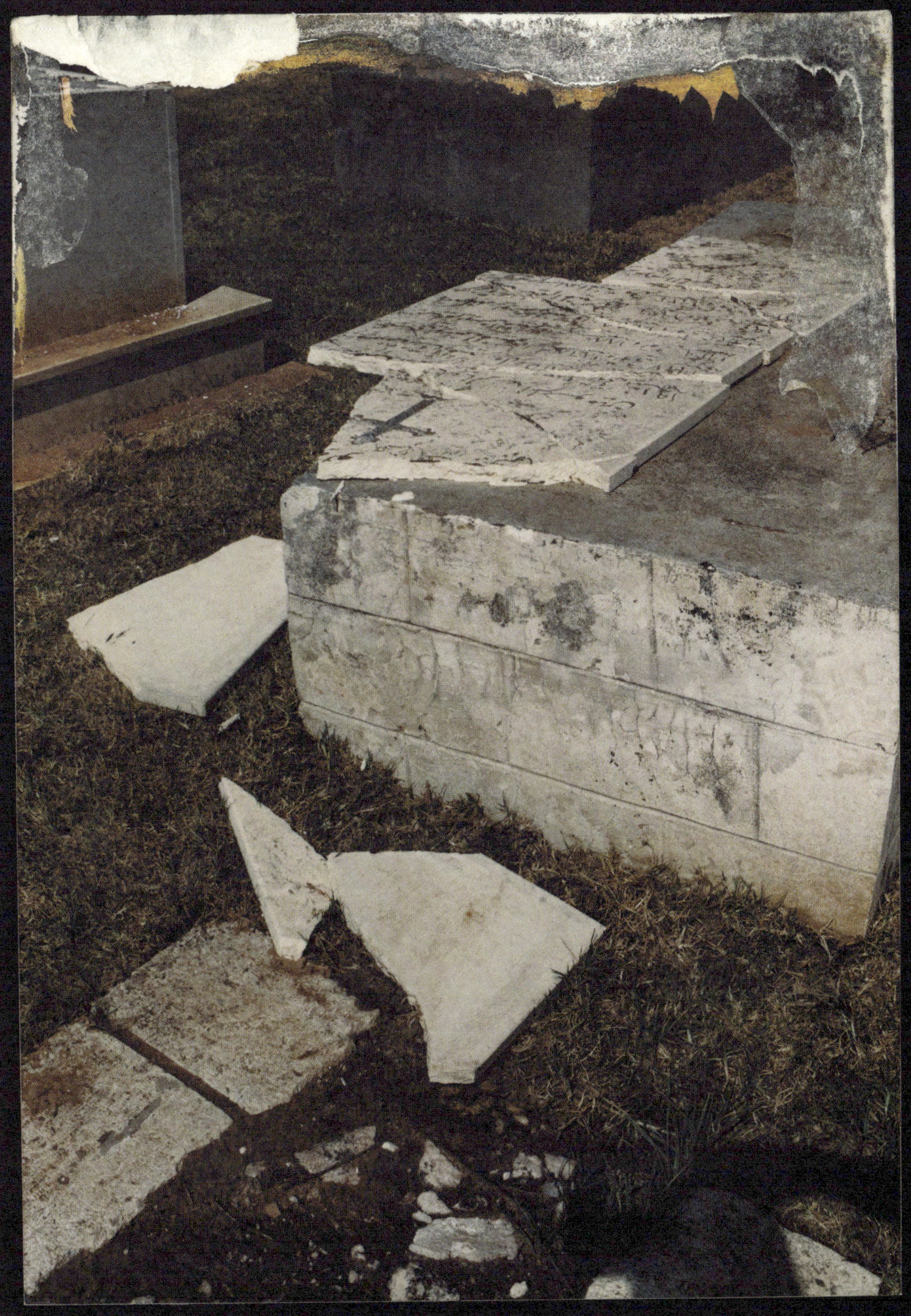

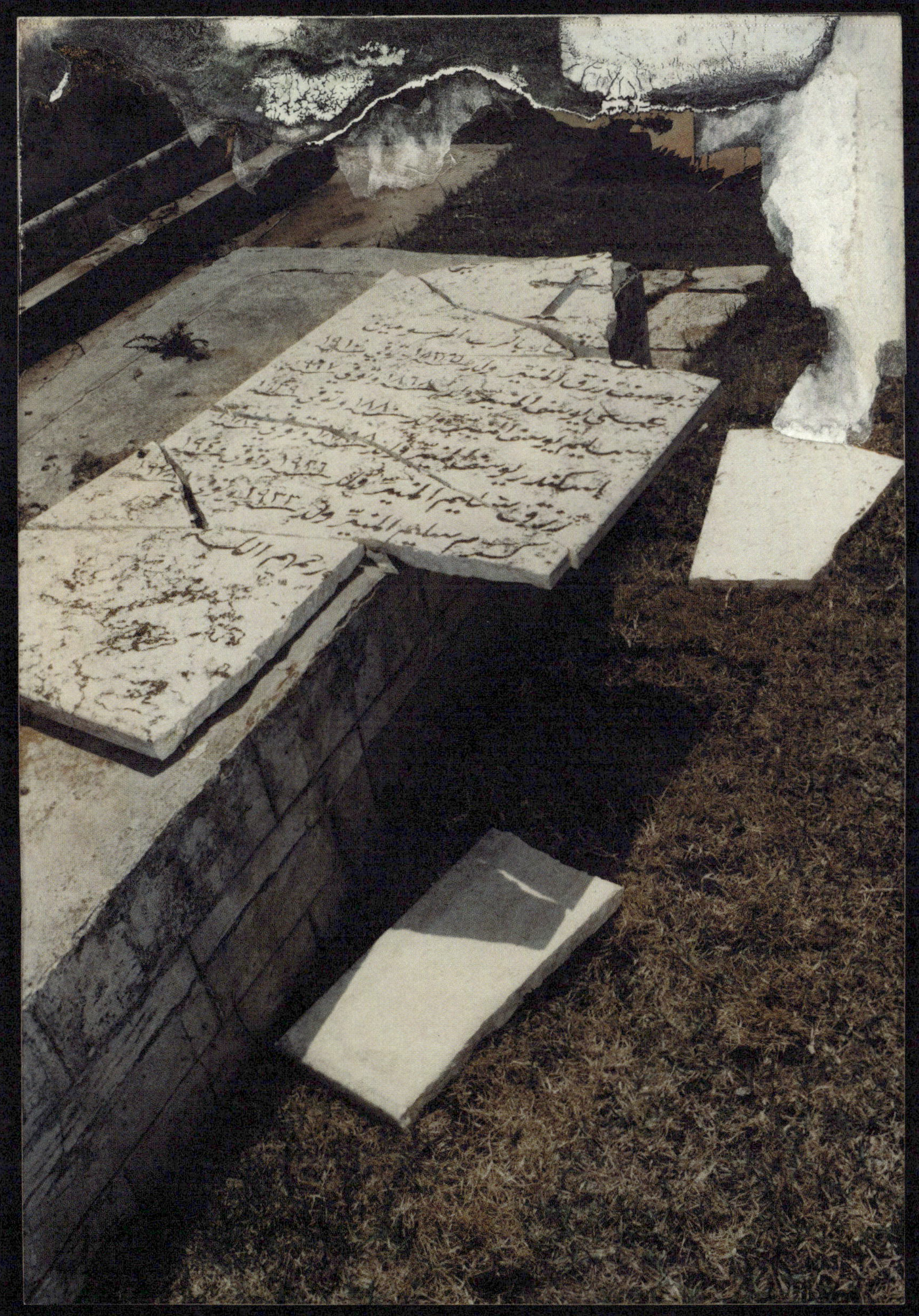

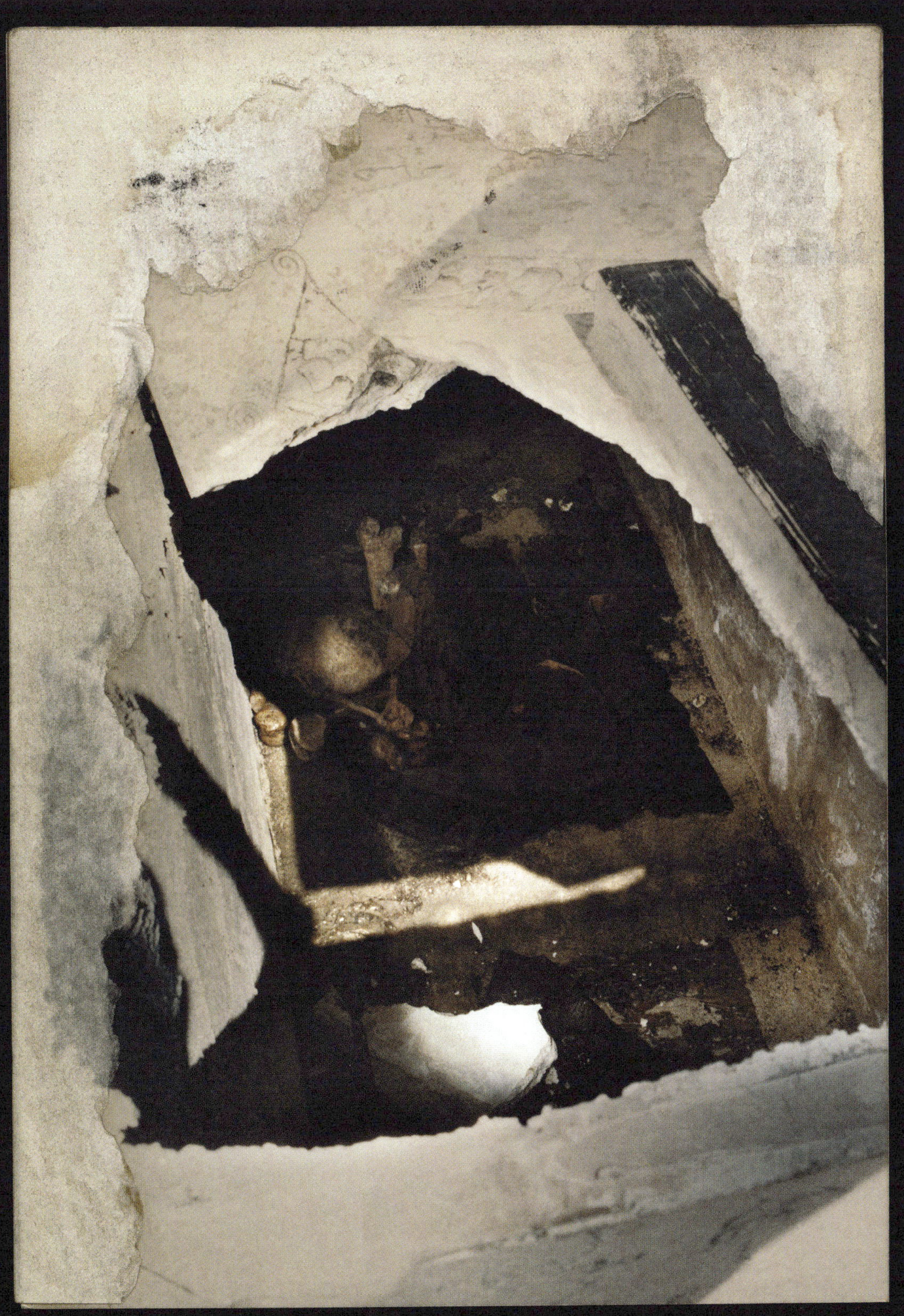

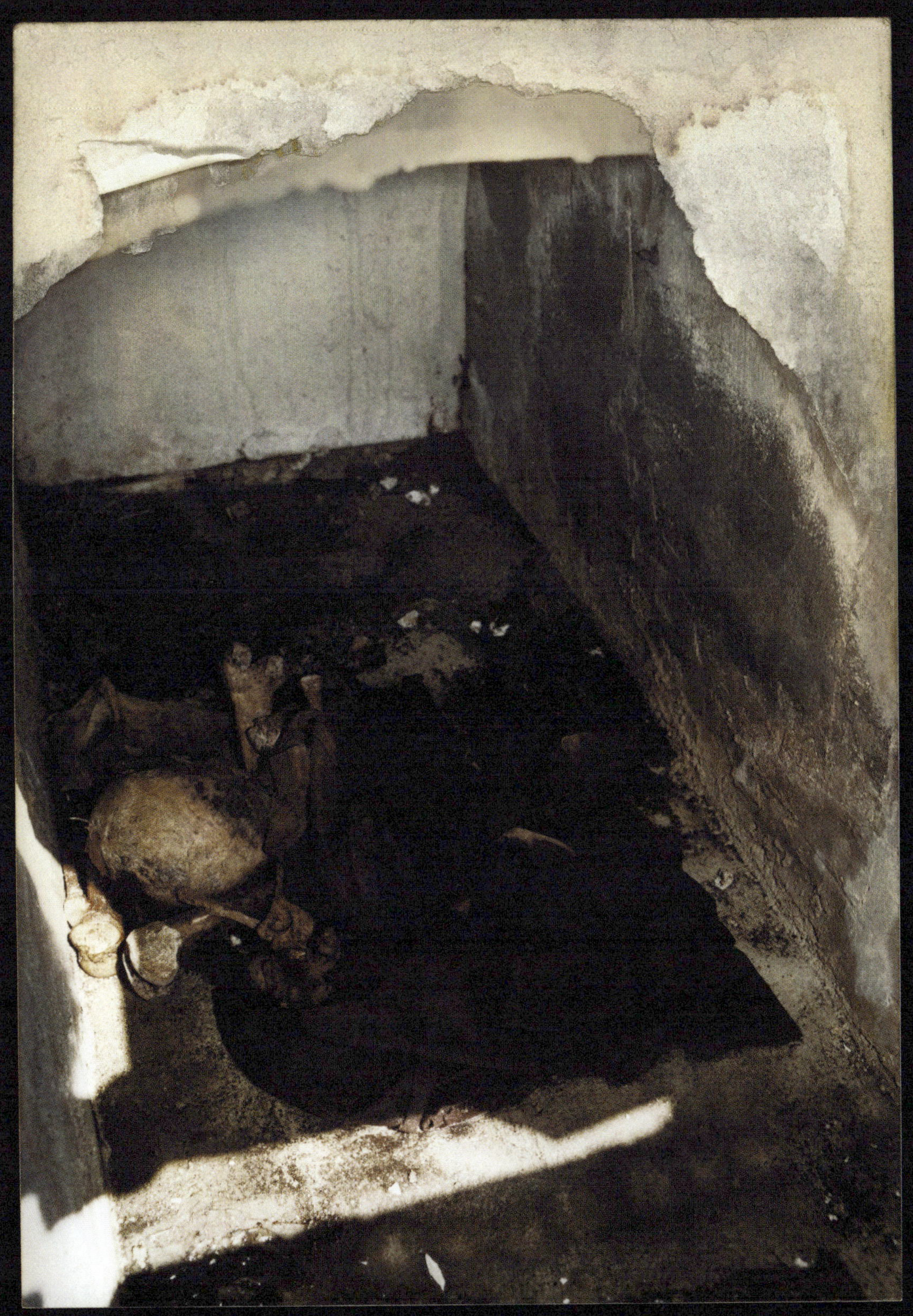

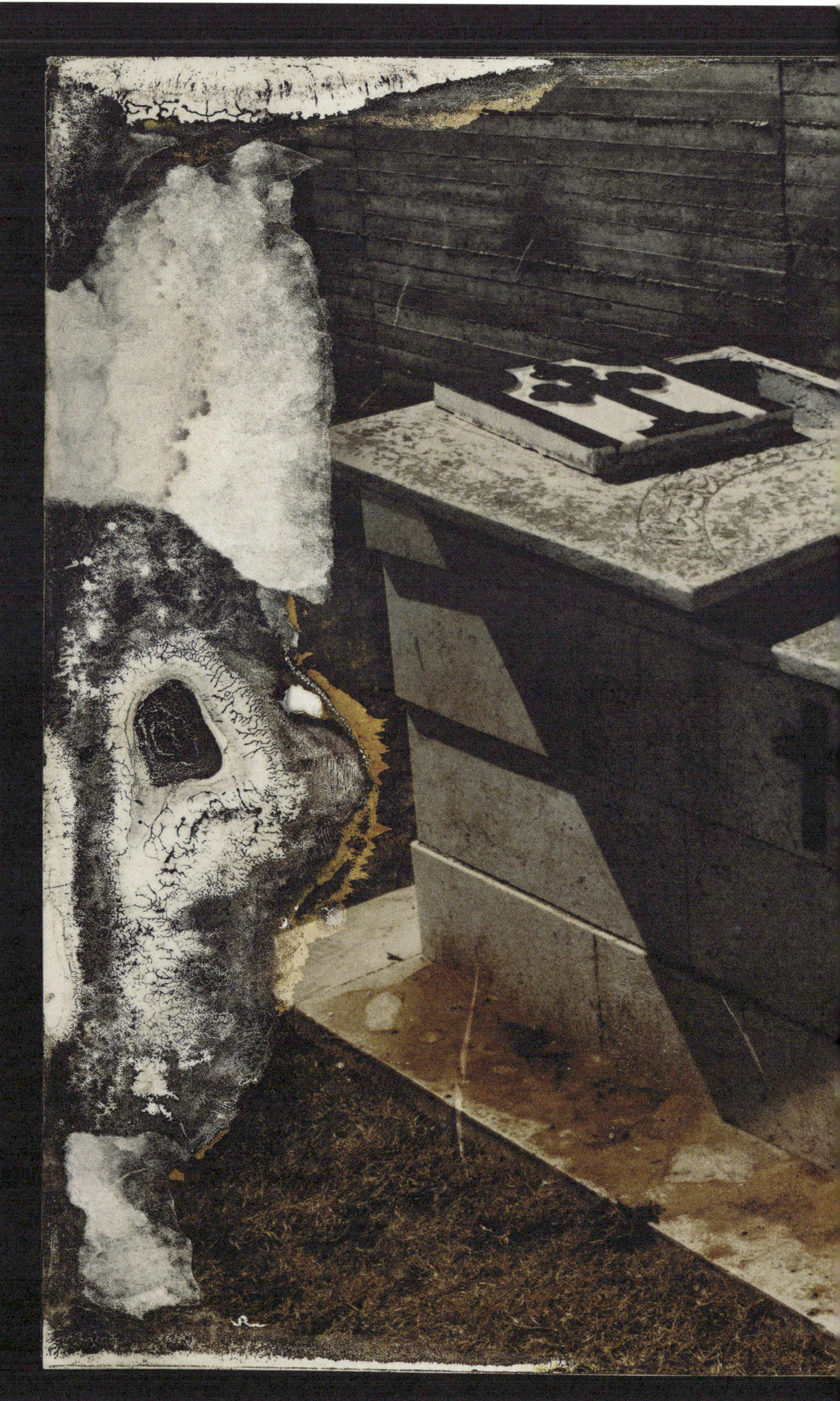

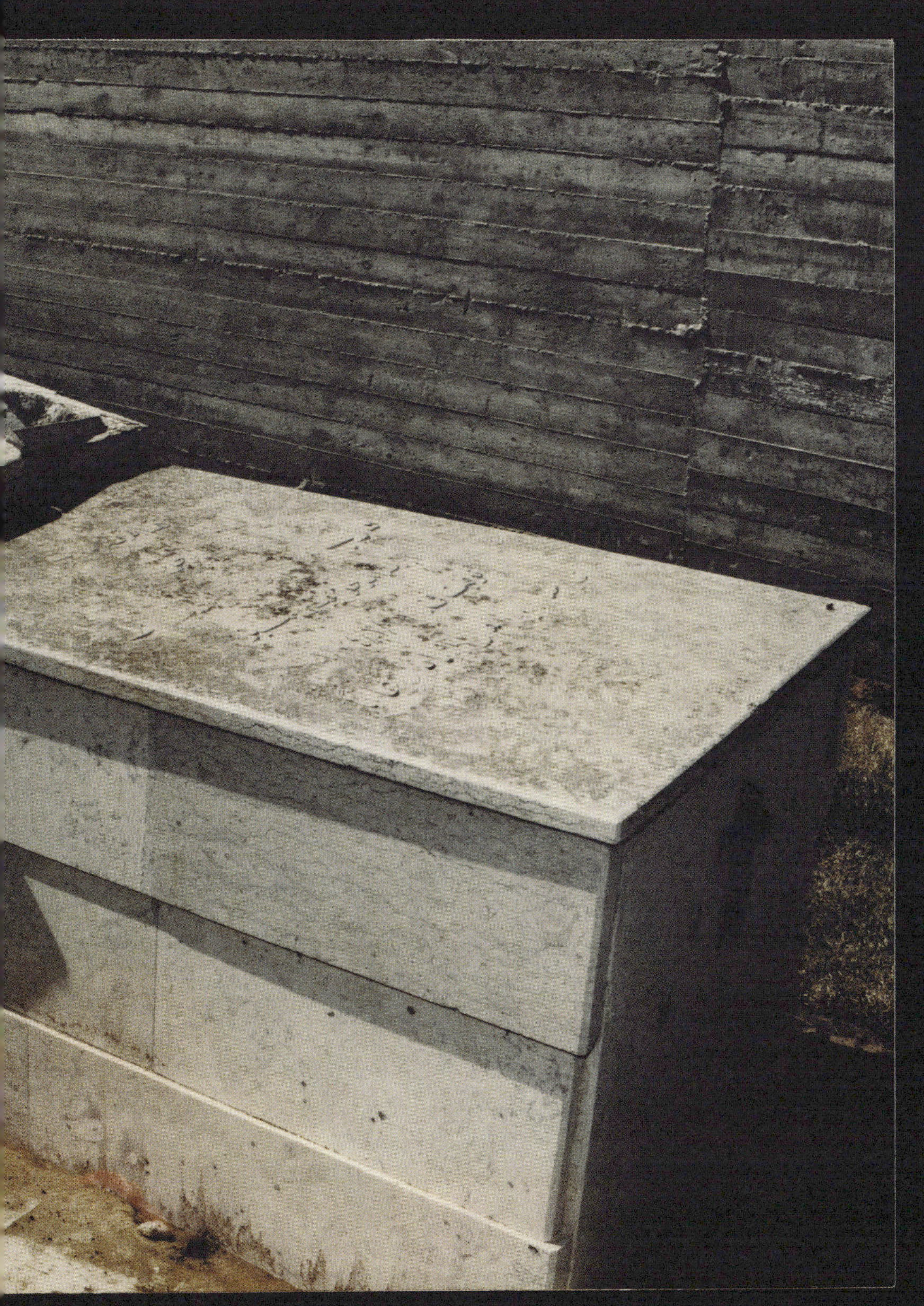

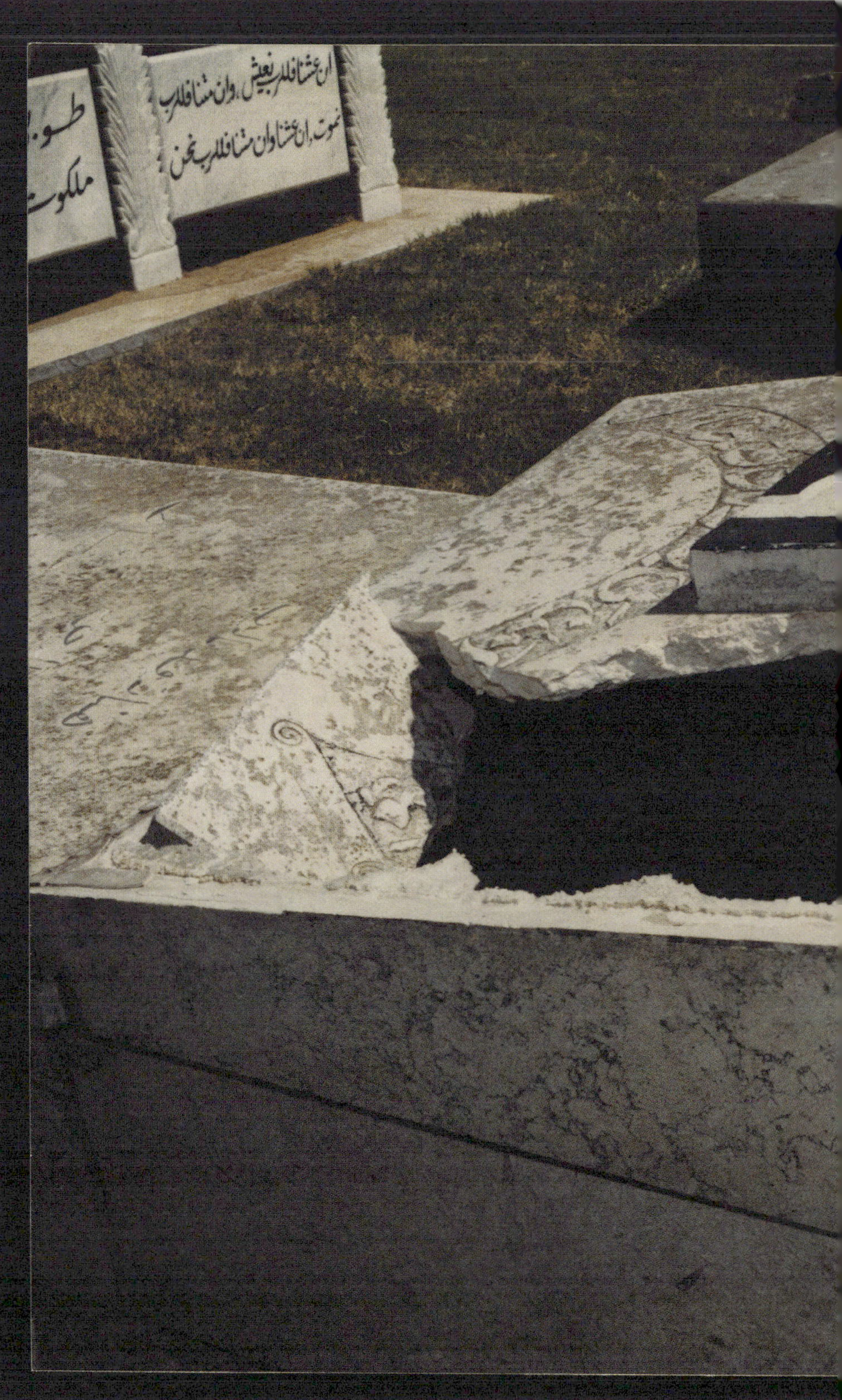

إن عشنا فللرب نعيش، وإن متنا فللرب
نموت، إن عشنا وإن متنا فللرب نحن
طو
ملكوت

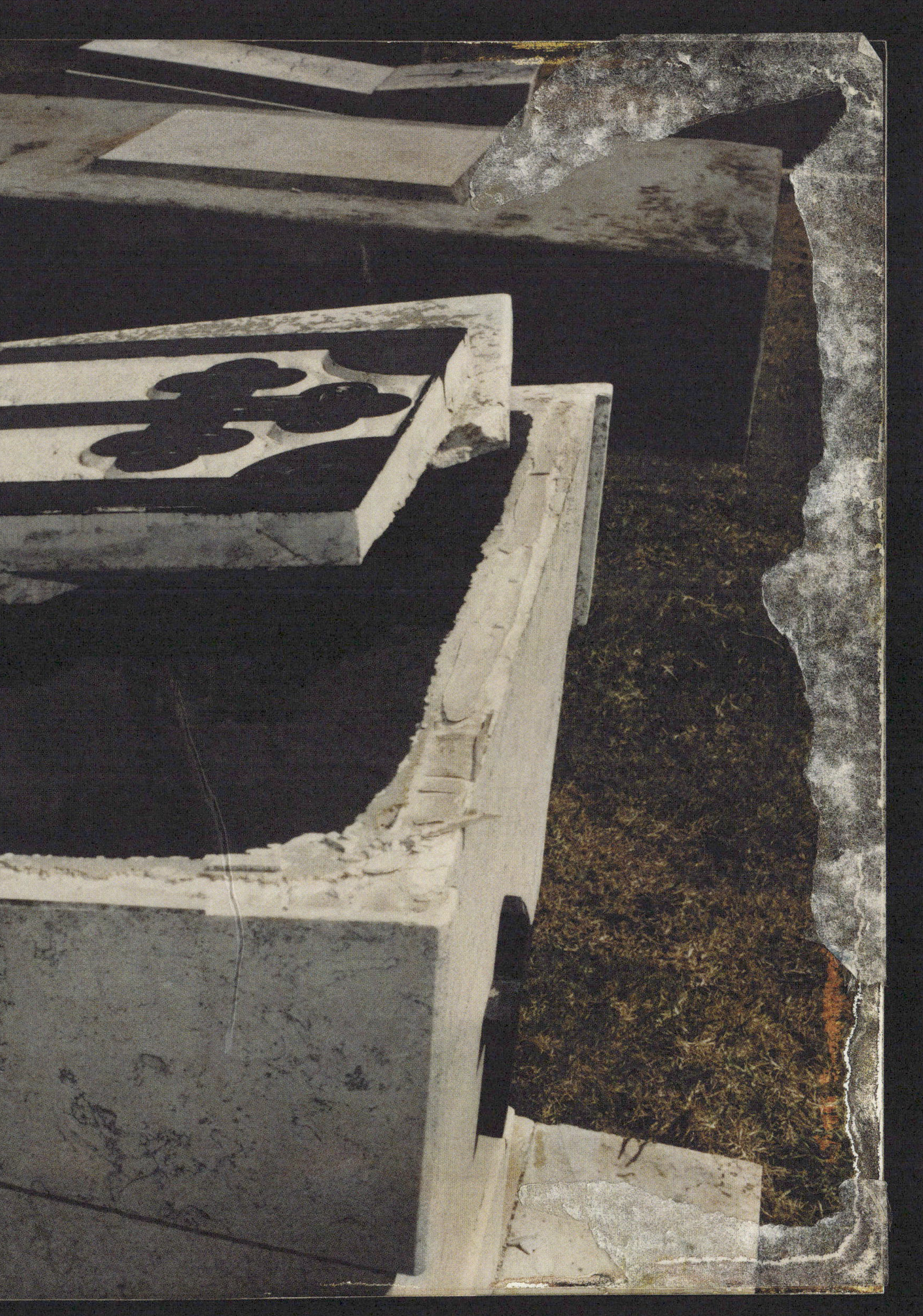

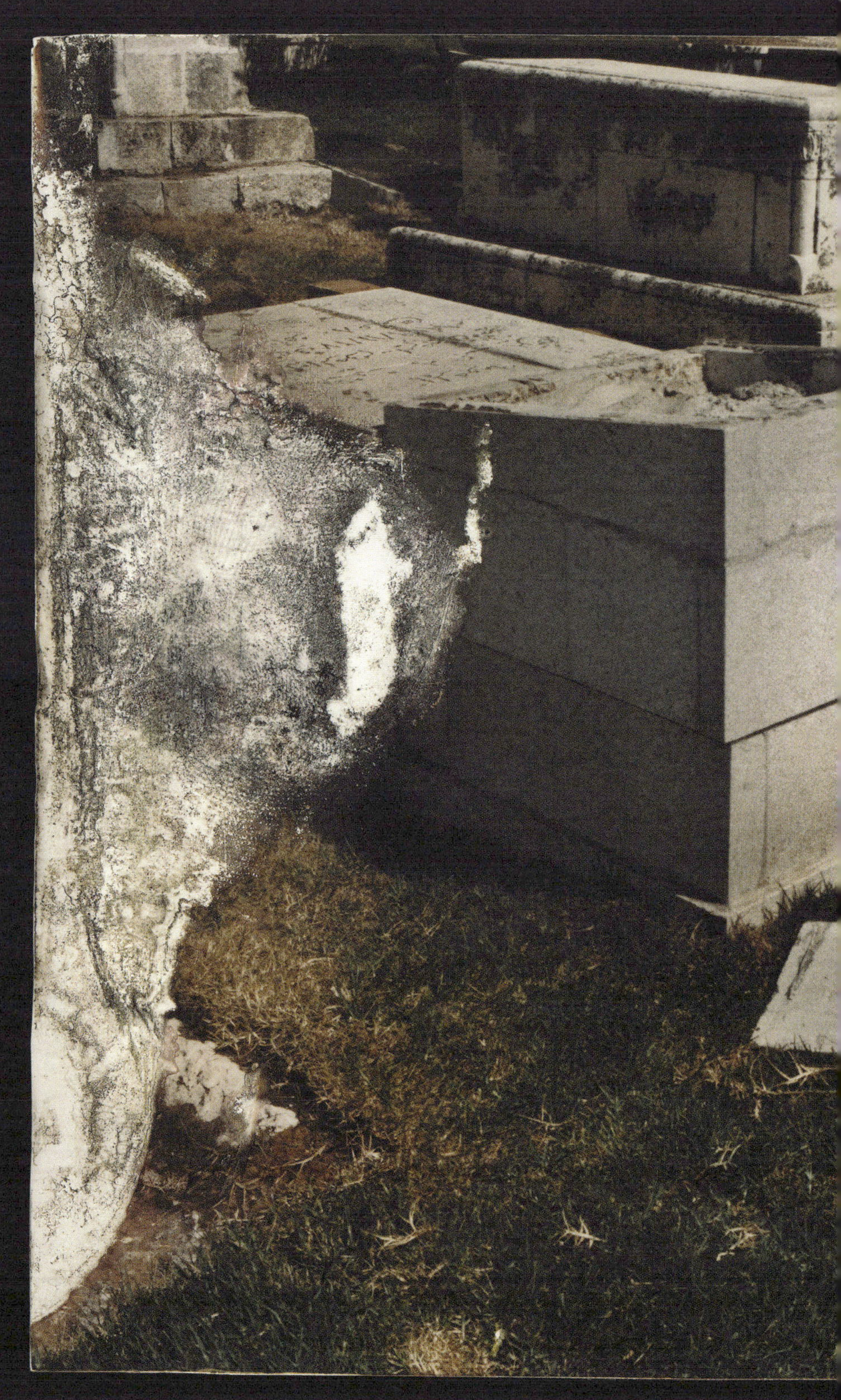

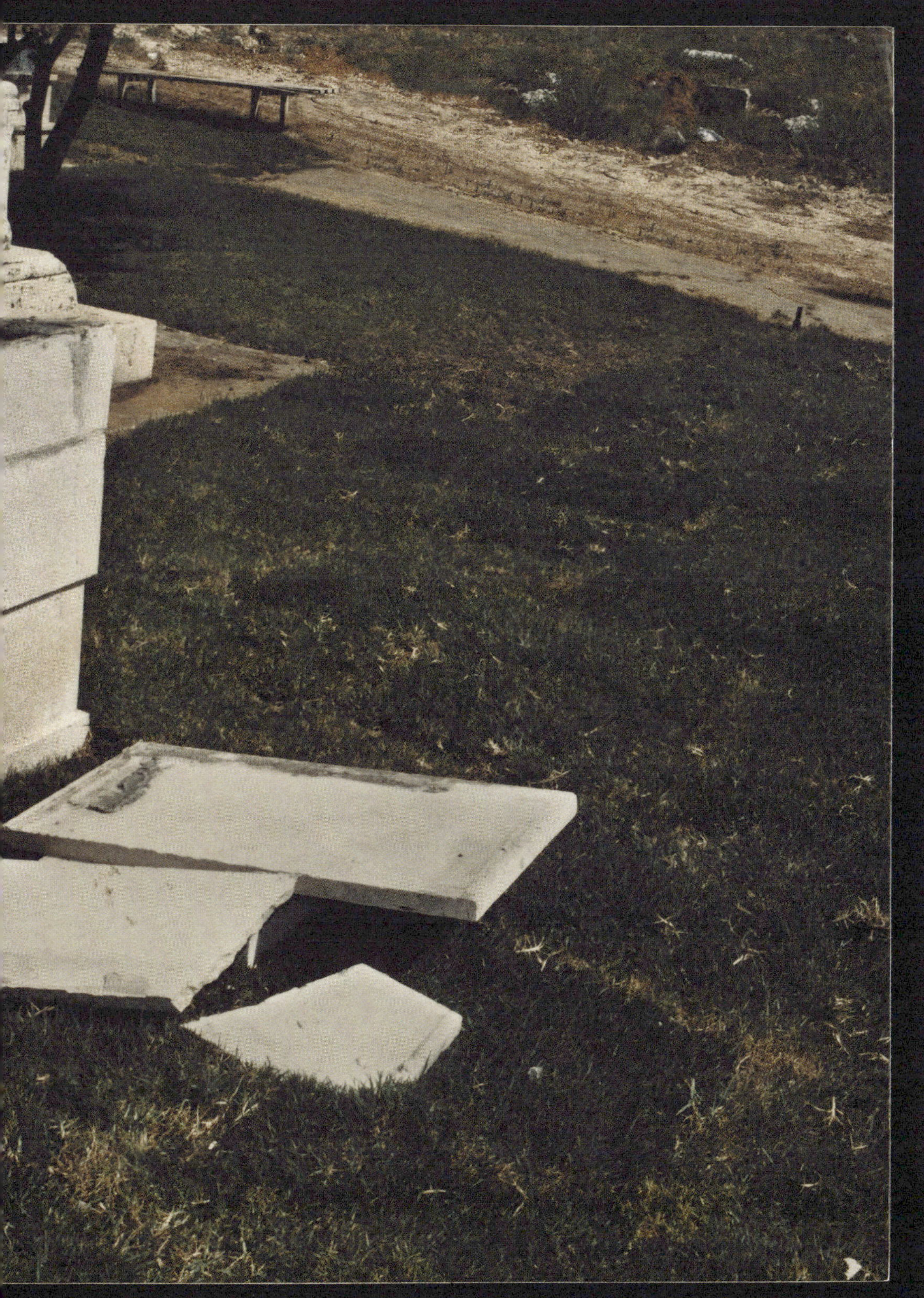

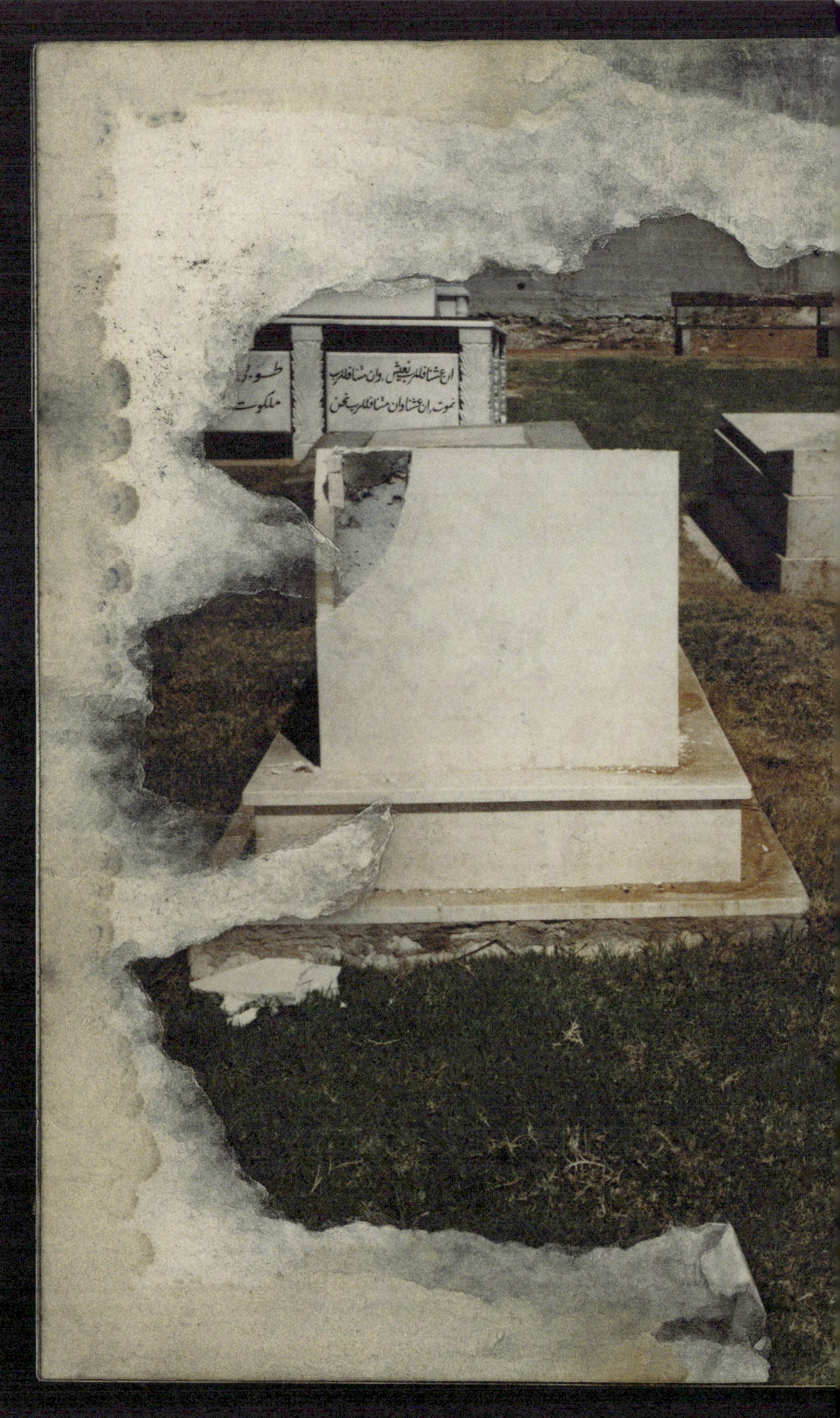

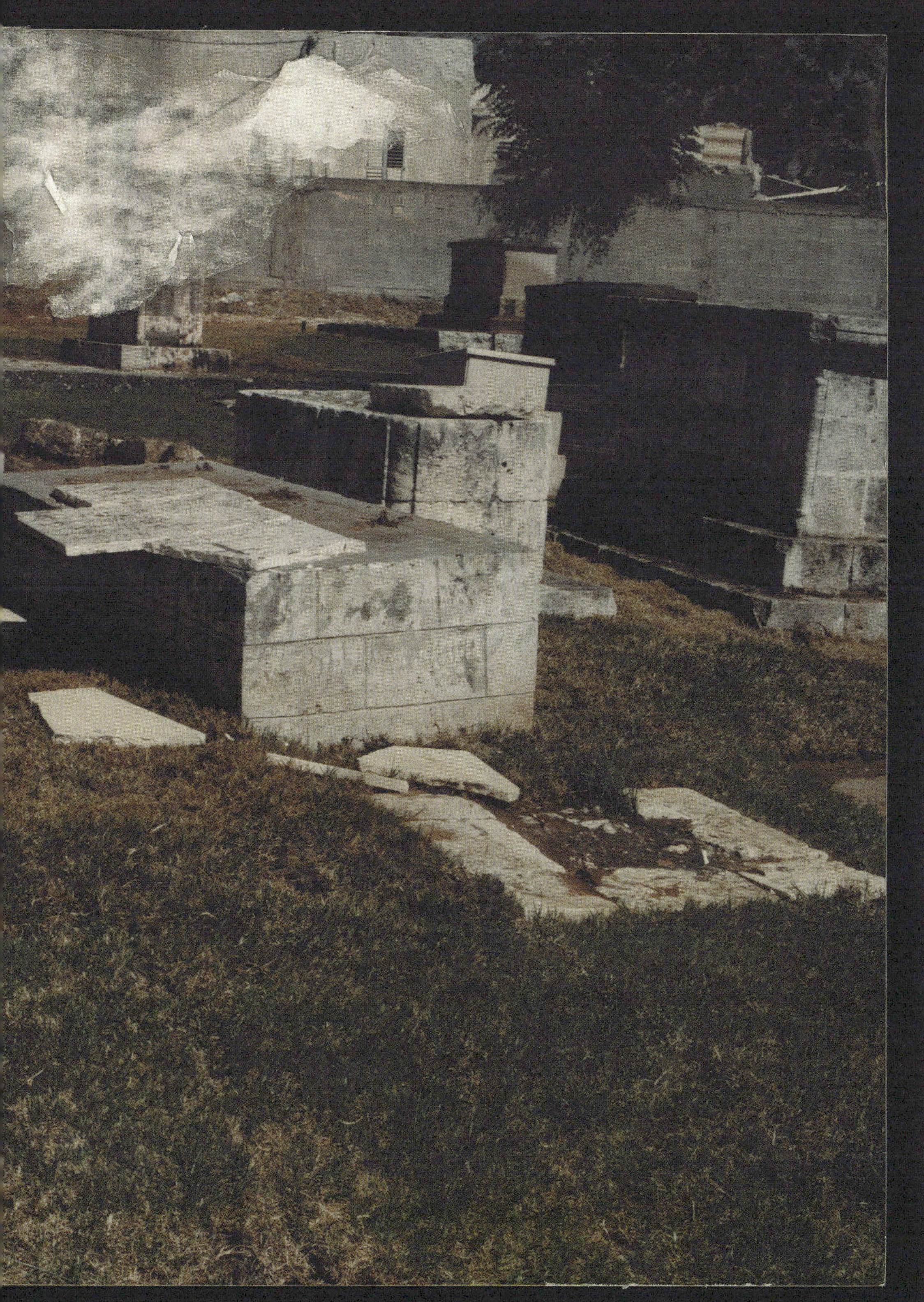

40 Days, Two-channel video installation, 15 min, 2012

40 يوماً، فيديو على قناتين ، 15 دقيقة ، 2012

And how is Jacob?

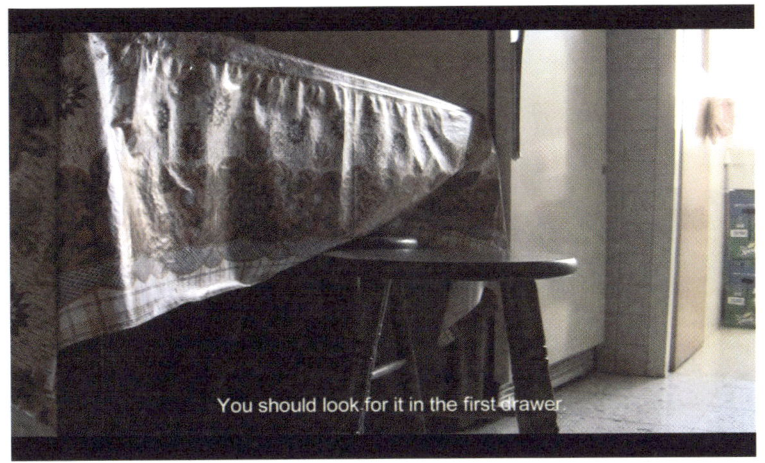

You should look for it in the first drawer.

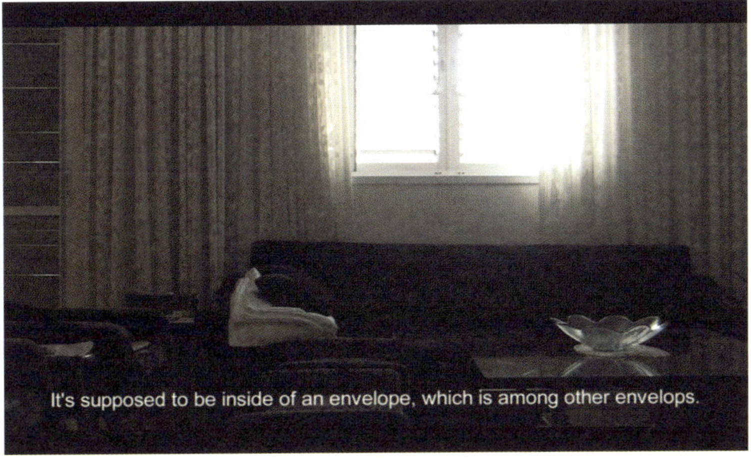

It's supposed to be inside of an envelope, which is among other envelops.

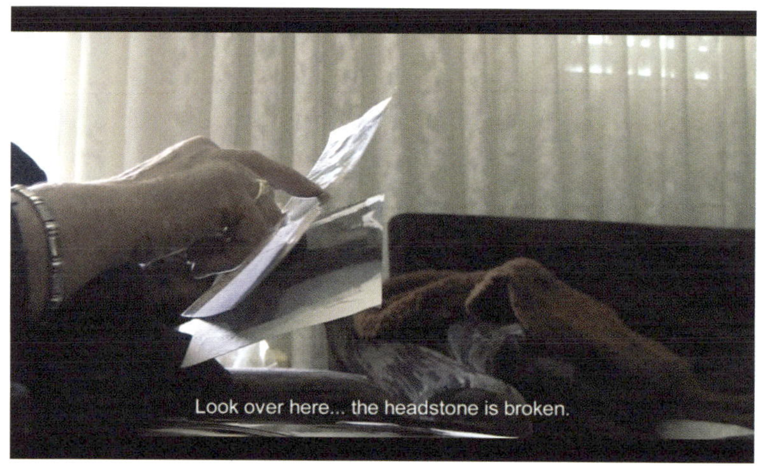
Look over here... the headstone is broken.

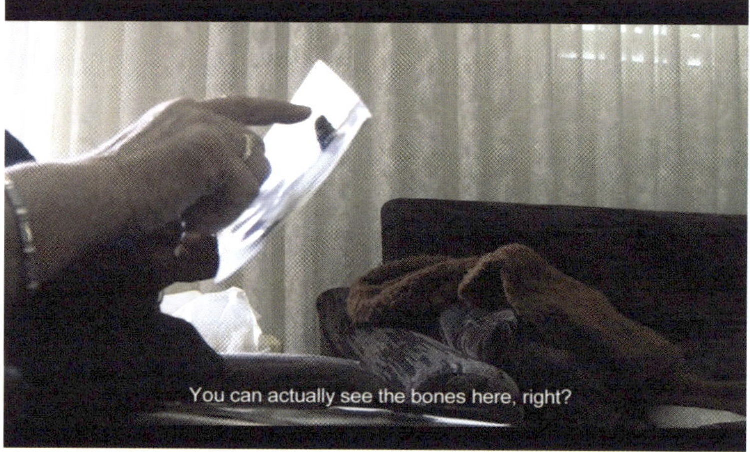
You can actually see the bones here, right?

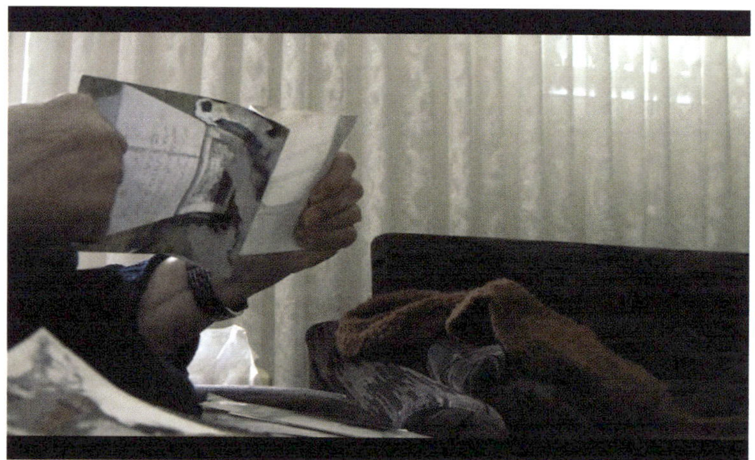

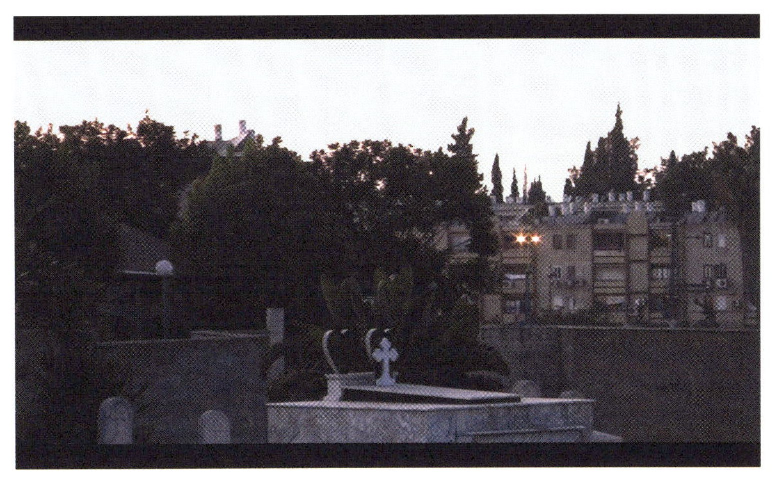

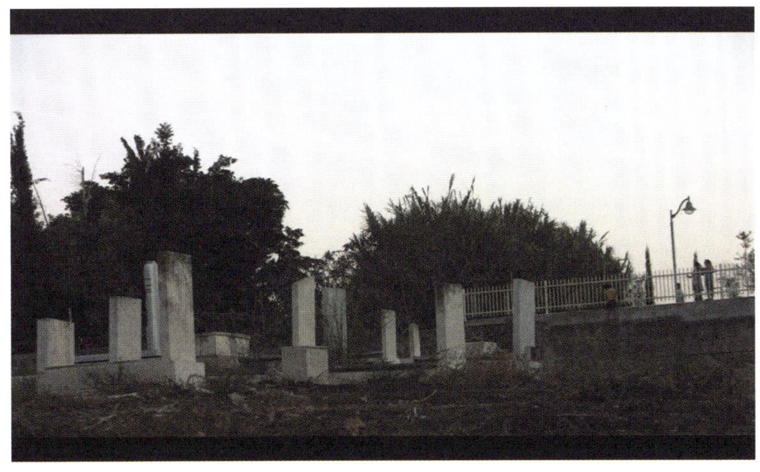

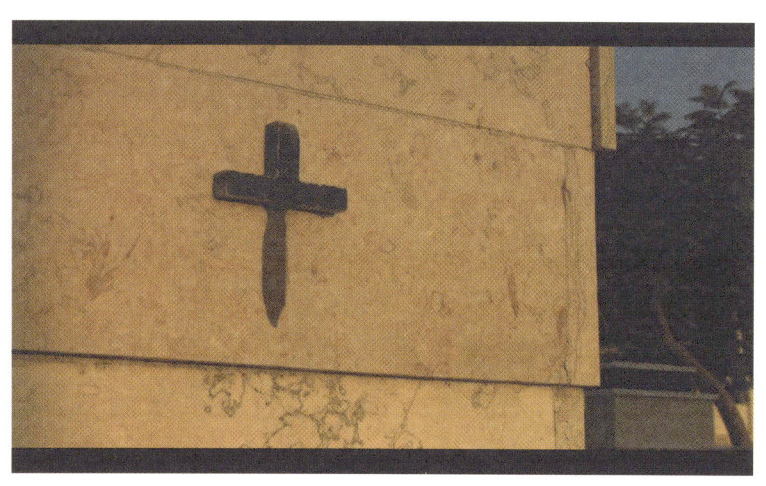

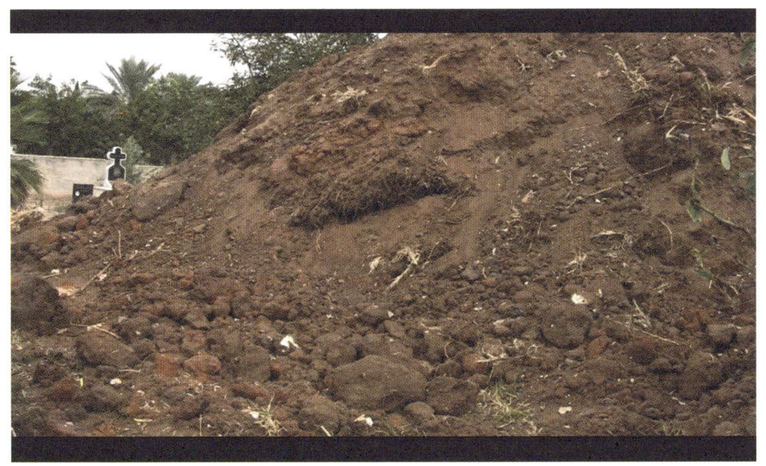

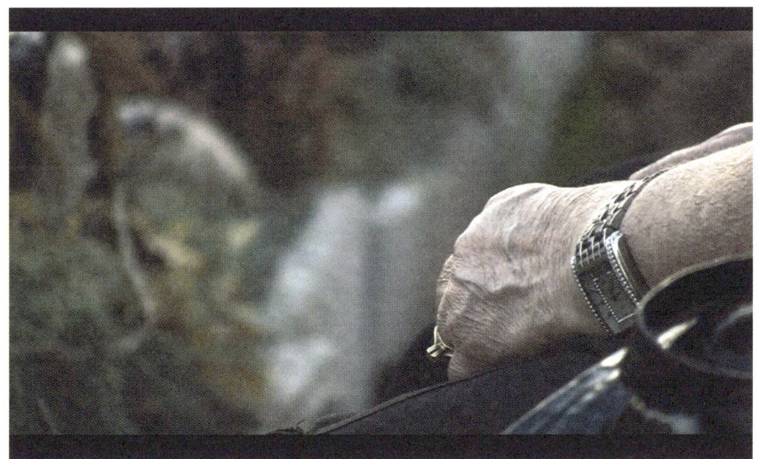

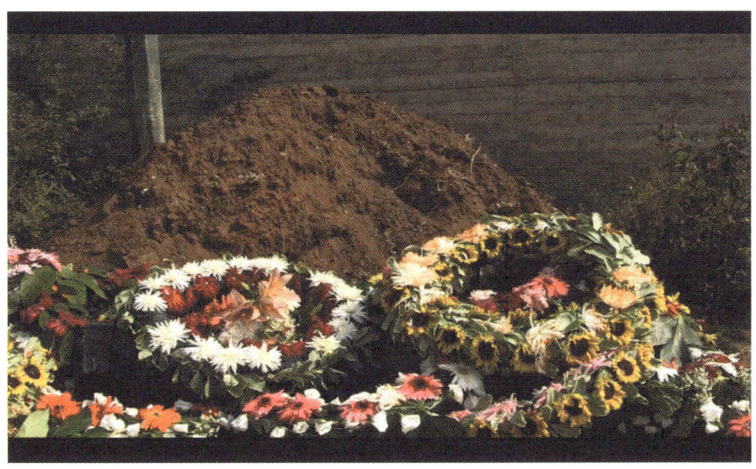

In 40 days

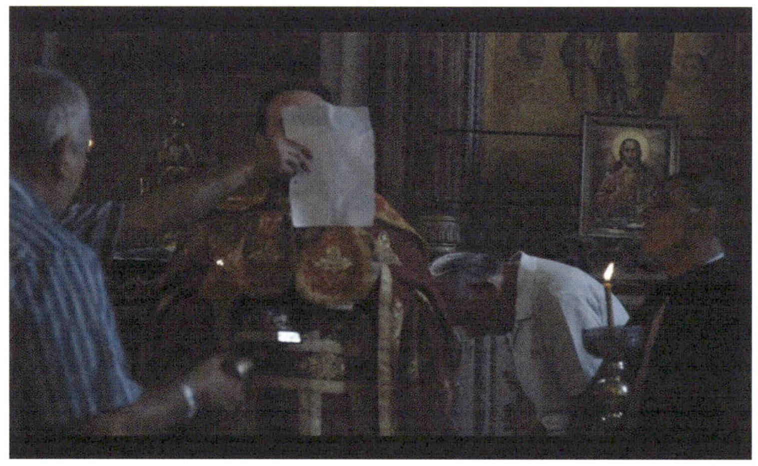

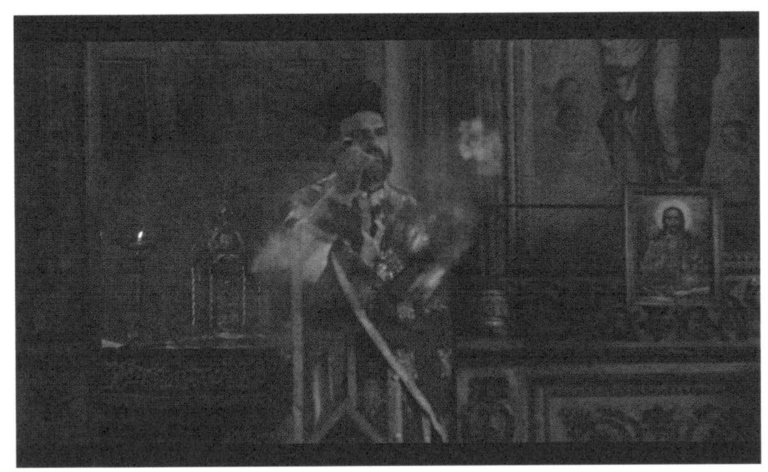

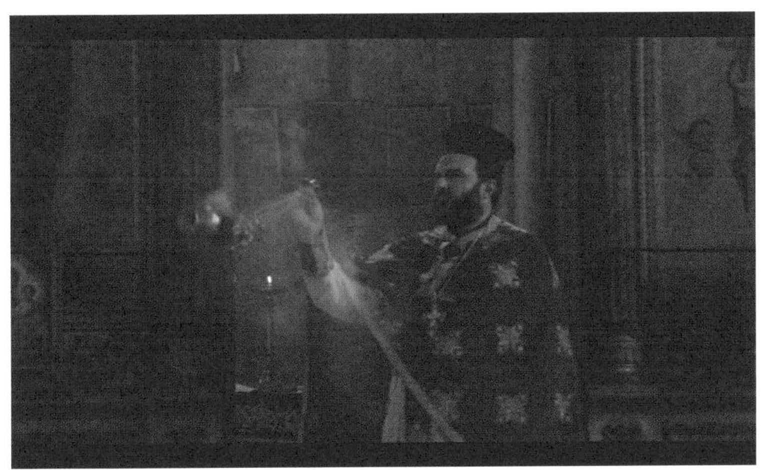

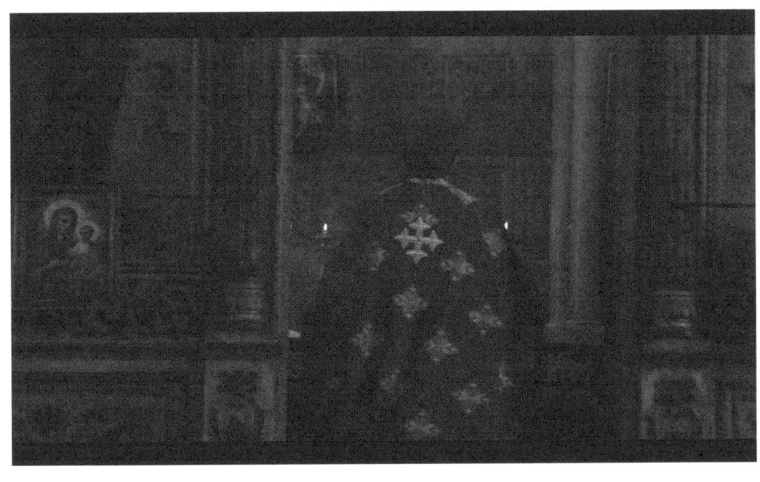

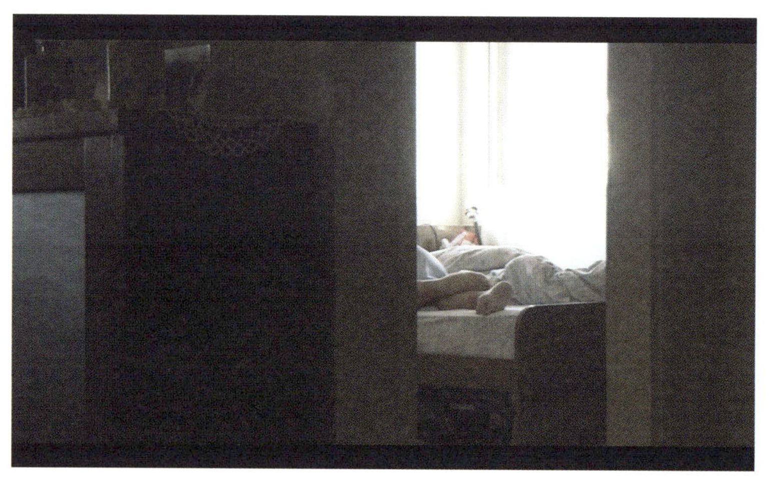

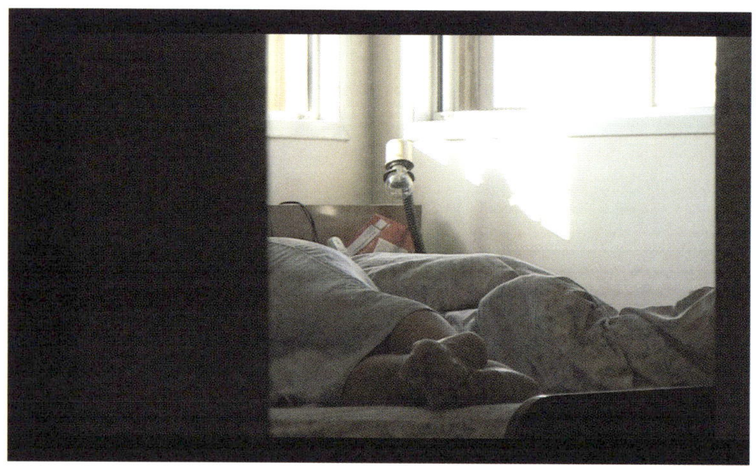

دور غويز: السيرة الذاتية

ولد دور غويز في القدس، وهو فنان متعدد التخصصات تتنوع تركيباته الفنية من الفيديو إلى التصوير الفوتوغرافي. وهو محاضر في دائرة التاريخ والنظرية في أكاديمية بيزاليل للفنون والتصميم بالقدس، وباحث في الأرشيفات بجامعة تل أبيب. وفي العام 2009، أنشأ أول أرشيف مكرس للأقلية المسيحية ـ الفلسطينية في الشرق الأوسط.

تشتمل معارض غويز المنفردة على عمل ”جيورجيوبوليس“ في متحف بيتاح تيكفا للفنون؛ و‘‘عائلة منيّر‘‘ في المتحف اليهودي، بنيويورك؛ و‘‘اللد‘‘ في معهد كنست ويرك للفن المعاصر، برلين؛ و‘‘كروم الوطن‘‘ في متحف تل أبيب للفن، وغاليري كارليه جيباور، برلين؛ و‘‘عكس التيار‘‘ في مركز بوششوبرغ للفنون، بروكسل، و‘‘سابر‘‘ في غاليري دفير، تل أبيب، و‘‘40 يوماً في جاليري آرت سبيس‘‘، سان أنتونيو، وغيرها. وحمل آخر عمل لغويز عنوان ”100 خطوة إلى البحر المتوسط‘‘، وقد تم عرضه في متحف روز للفنون في بوسطن. كذلك عرض عمله في بينالي اسطنبول الثاني عشر؛ وفي مهرجان الفن المعاصر الدولي السابع عشر؛ وفيديو برازيل، في ساو باولو؛ وبينالي موسكو الدولي الثالث؛ وقصر طوكيو، في باريس؛ وبينالي بينين؛ وبينالي بوخارست، ومتحف ميتروبوليتان طوكيو للتصوير وغيرها.

وحاز غويز على منحة أورغلير من جامعة تل أبيب؛ وجائزة ناثان برلموتر للإقامة الفنية، عن متحف روز للفنون، في جامعة برانديس؛ وجائزة الإقامة الفنية الدولية، من آرت سبيس، سان أنتونيو.

على لحظات حاسمة، لكنها بكماء أيضاً، ومعانيها الصامتة تبرز في الفراغ القائم ما بين الصورة والناظر إليها. كذلك، فإن السياق التاريخي المروّع والعرض الأرشيفي يعيدان لهذه الصورة الفوتوغرافية صوتها مثلما كتبت: ''هذه صورة غيتو لود''.

تم نشر هذه المقالة للمرة الأولى في كتاب دور غويز ـ مائة خطوة الى المتوسط ، دار نيوانجلند للنشر، ٢١٠٢

1 ''الغائبـ الحاضر''، تعبير رسمي استخدم لتحديد الفلسطينيين الذين بقوا في الوطن بعد العام 1948، لكن أراضيهم وأملاكهم جرت مصادرتها وسلمت إلى الدولة. إذ أن ''قانون ملكية الغائب'' للعام 1950، يمنح دولة إسرائيل الأصول التي تعود لهؤلاء الفلسطينيين المهجرين منها خلال حرب العام 1948.

2 تعبير ''غيتو'' يعود إلى الحي اليهودي خلال القرن السادس عشر في فينيسيا (البندقية)، وهي المنطقة الوحيدة في المدينة التي كان مسموحاً لليهود أن يعيشوا فيها. واسمها مشتق من (غيتو في لهجة سكانها) وتعني ''محددة''. وبعد ذلك أصبح تعبير ''غيتو'' يستخدم لكل الأحياء اليهودية في أوروبا. واليوم أصبح التعبير يشير إلى جزء من المدينة الخاص بالمجاميع الإثنية أو الى الموقع الاجتماعي والاقتصادي المتدني.

3 حايم يعقوبي:

The Jewish-Arab City: Spatio-Politics in a Mixed Community
(London: Routledge, 2009), 32, 61

4 يعتبر طرد إسرائيل للمدنيين الفلسطينيين العام 1948، ومصادرة أملاكهم، وإنكار حق عودتهم بعد الحرب، ممارسات تحرمها اتفاقية جنيف (4) المعنية بحماية المدنيين في وقت الحرب. جنيف، 21 آب 1948، الفقرتان 94 و53 (انظر الرابط:
www.icrc.org/ihl.nsf/FULL/380?OpenDocument, accessed 6/3/12

لذلك، فإن التصوير الفوتوغرافي والذاكرة يتشابكان بطرائق مختلفة. فالصور الفوتوغرافية قادرة على التنافس مع الذكريات المعاشة غير الموثقة، بل وتجبرها على التكيف معها أو تناقضها أو تؤكدها. أنا لم أنظر أبداً إلى صور عرس خالي خوفاً على ما تحمله الصور من جمال في ذاكرتي، وأنها قد لا تستطيع الوقوف أمام اختبار الزمن أو تغير الأذواق، وما يمكن للصور الفوتوغرافية أن تقوضه من التجربة الشخصية. مع ذلك، فإنه من المعتاد تصوير المناسبات السعيدة مثل الأعراس وترتيب الصور الفوتوغرافية في ألبومات. ووضع الكاميرات اليوم يرفع من درجة الإدراك بين المشاركين في تلك المناسبة، بأنها ستُذكر ويعاد النظر إليها مستقبلاً من خلال الصور الفوتوغرافية الملتقطة، وتلك الأكثر أهمية غالباً ما تؤطَّر وتعرض في أماكن تكريم خاصة.

كان حفل زواج جديًّ أول عرس فلسطيني يجري في اللد بعد العام 1948. ودون أن يعلما، نقلت صور عرسهما دور التذكارات العائلية إلى مستوى أعلى وأصبحت مشحونة بأهمية تاريخية باعتبارها دليلاً أرشيفياً نادراً عن الحياة في ''غيتو لود''.

بعد أن شغّلت جدتي مصوراً ووقفت أمامه لتصويرها ودفعت للصور واستلمتها، قامت بعزلها جميعاً في كيس بلاستيكي، دفنته تحت السرير. لماذا لم تنظم الصور في ألبوم، مثلما كانت العادة وما زالت؟ إن السياق التاريخي يقدم مفتاحاً لفهم هذا السلوك المتناقض. فالمرء لا يعرض الصور التي تعد إهانة في ألبوم عائلي.

في ذلك العام، باشرت بمشروع ما زال قائماً، إنه الأرشيف المسيحي الفلسطيني. ويبدأ بالصور الموجودة في مسلسل ''سكانوغرامات # 1''، التي تشير إلى الممارسة المتمثلة في تجميع ألبومات عائلية. ويضم الأرشيف صوراً تعتبر عادة أنواعاً فوتوغرافية منقرضة مثل ''صور الجواز الفوتوغرافية''، و''صور الأعراس الفوتوغرافية''، و''صور الصفوف الفوتوغرافية''. الوثائق في الأرشيف لم تؤخذ من ألبومات عائلية، بل تم جمعها من أكياس بلاستيكية مبعثرة في اللد، وعمان، ولندن والقاهرة، ونيقوسيا. أما صورة سميرة منيّر الملتقطة ''بعد سنة على العام 1948''، فهي ليست ضمن ألبوم عرس جدتي، وليست هي مجرد صورة لحفل زواجها. إنها دليل على نكبتها.[4] فالصور غالباً ما توصف بأنها تقبض

لها. هناك مسافة محددة تفصل ما بين العروس والكاميرا. إنها مسافة يلتزم بها الجميع ضمناً، ولا أحد يقوم بتجاوزها.

وجدت صور عرس جديَّ العام 2009 في كيس بلاستيكي أبيض داخل حقيبة ملابس بالية محفوظة تحت سريرهما، على جانب النصف الذي يحتله جدي من السرير. "هذه هي صور عرسنا"، أكدت جدتي بعد ستين سنة مرت على التقاطها. سألتها: "في أي سنة؟" فأجابت، بذهن شارد: "بعد سنة الـ 1948"، وكأنها كانت تريد إقصاء ذلك من حلقات الزمن، تكيفاً مع تقويم داخلي خاص بها. كانت عائلة جدتي قد أجبرت على الفرار من يافا العام 1948، ولم تعد أبداً إلى بيتها. وهذا كل ما أعرفه. وهكذا، تركتها على حالها ولم أطرح عليها أسئلة أخرى.

في فترة لاحقة من ذلك العام، وخلال تصويري لفيديو "يوليو 13"، سمعت جدي يستخدم عبارة "غيتو لود" للمرة الأولى، فذهلت. كانت كلمة "غيتو" تحمل في ذهني معاني مختلفة لها علاقة بالأحياء الفقيرة أو بتاريخ يهود أوروبا الشرقية.[2] لكن جدي ظل يكرر: "غيتو لود". بحثت في جوجل عن هذه العبارة فظهر لي سؤال يصحح ما كتبته: "هل تعني غيتو لودز (المدينة البولونية)؟" عرفت بعد ذلك أن الاسم قد أعطي من قبل الحكومة التي تشكلت في إسرائيل بعد حرب العام 1948، للمنطقة المسيّجة الممتدة حول كنيسة القديس على الخروج في اللد. بعد احتلال المدينة على يد الجيش الإسرائيلي في تموز 1948، أجبرت أغلبية سكانها الفلسطينيين للخروج مشياً على الأقدام إلى المنفى.

ولم يبقَ في مدينة اللد سوى 1030 فلسطينياً، وهؤلاء جمعوا في مساحة صغيرة محاطة بالأسلاك الشائكة تحت الحكم العسكري، ومنع التجول وأطلق عليها اسم: غيتو لود. ويعود هذا التعبير الى الحي الذي لجأ اليه أولئك السكان والمهاجرون الفلسطينيون الفارون من قرى مجاورة، الذين استقروا في اللد بعد العام 1948، وحتى اليوم تسمى تلك المنطقة من المدينة باسم "غيتو".[3]

مع مرور الوقت، تبدأ الصور الفوتوغرافية بتشويش الصور المحفورة في أذهاننا، لتصبح في الأخير الممثل البصري الرسمي لتلك المناسبات. أما المناسبات غير الموثقة، تغرق في أغلب الأحيان داخل بحر اللاشعور.

اليوم الذي كنا نذهب فيه إلى الشاطئ خلال موسم الصيف. وفي صباح ذلك السبت غير المؤرخ، أخذتني جدتي مع أخي إلى شاطئ يافا، المدينة التي ولدتْ فيها العام 1932، حيث يقع بيت طفولتها على بعد 100 خطوة من شاطئ البحر المتوسط. هي لم تكن تسكن في يافا، لكنها في صباح ذلك السبت حملتني إلى البحر، واتّخذت من ظهرها طوافة لي. كان البحر هادئاً. وكانت جدتي، الصغيرة الحجم، ترتدي ثوب سباحة أسود، وشعرت آنذاك كأني أركب على ظهر حوت. وتحت شعور جارف بالأمن ممزوجاً بالإثارة، التفتّ إلى الوراء لأتطلع إلى شاطئ يافا، فبدت لي البيوت المطلية بلون التراب صغيرة جداً على المنحدر البعيد.

بعد عقود عدة، وجدت نفسي أتفحص صورة لعرس جدتي. وكانت قد التقطت على يد مصور لم تستطع تذكر اسمه. كان وجهها مغطى بطرحة عرس من الشيفون الشفاف، مع ذلك، كان ممكناً مشاهدة عينيها تحدقان في الكاميرا من وراء الطرحة. كانت شفتاها المطليتان مكتومتين، وتشبه ملامحها ملامح أمي. إنها شابة وترتدي ثوب زفاف أبيض، يفصلها عن الحشد ويسلط الانتباه إليها. إنها حضور غائب.[1]

إلى يسارها تقف نينا أقرب صديقاتها، وأخوها جاك، الذي كان أكثر نحافة ووسامة من الرجل الذي أتذكره من طفولتي. وهي محاطة بإشبيناتها اللواتي لبسن أحسن ما لديهن، وكان شعرهن مسرحاً ومزيناً بشرائط، وهناك بنت عمها روجيت إلى يمينها، وأخت العريس رويدة وراءها.

إنها مناسبة توثق عادةً: العروس، برفقة عائلتها وصديقاتها، تترك بيتها وتذهب إلى مكان عام، لدعوة سكان المدينة للمشاركة في الاحتفال. في الصورة امرأة مسلمة، عرفت من خلال غطاء رأسها الأسود، تقف ضمن الحشد، وهذا ما يؤكد أن أفراداً من ديانات أخرى كانوا يشاركون في احتفالات من هذا النوع. هناك امرأة قصيرة أخرى تقف في يمين الصورة، وتمد برقبتها إلى الأعلى، على أمل أن تكون ضمن الصورة. وفي يسارها هناك رجلان: توفيق، عم سميرة، الذي يسعى إلى جعل الكاميرا تواجه كل وجهه (من المؤسف، أن نصفه بقي مخفياً)؛ وعيسى، عم العريس، الذي يقف بشكل جانبي، مرتدياً طربوشاً عثمانياً وجلابية مخططة يرتدي فوقها سترة، وهو لا ينظر إلى الكاميرا. فهو في مهمة، تتمثل بالإعلان عن وصول العروس، والتقطِت الصورة لحظة انفتاح فمه، وهو يغني تكريماً

”هذه صورة غيتو لود“ لدور غويز

المكان والتاريخ: لود (اللد)، 1949
المناسبة: عرس سميرة ويعقوب منيّر
المصور: مجهول

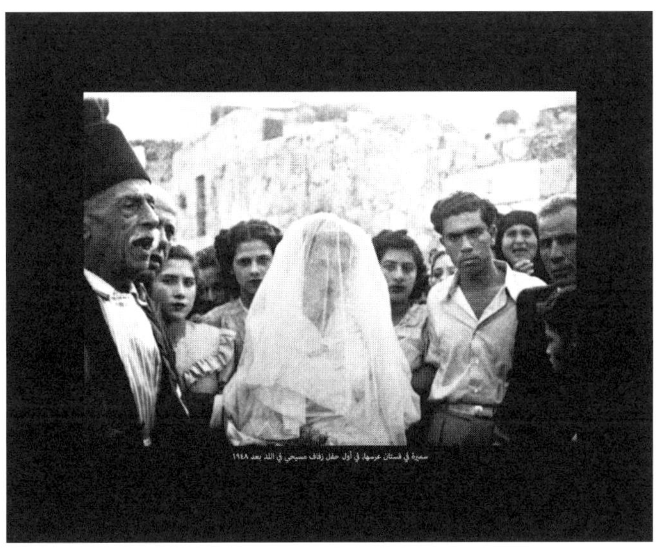

سكانوغرام رقم 1، صورة رقم 9، سميرة في ثوب عرسها، أول عرس فلسطيني مسيحي في مدينة الّد بعد العام 1948

تتنافس مناسبتان على احتلال أول ذكرياتي، أولاهما عرس خالي. كنت أيامها في الثالثة من عمري تقريباً. كانت أصابع عروسه مزينة بكشتبانات ملونة تتحرك بشكل إيقاعي على خلفية ثوب العرس الأبيض خلال رقصتها وقد حفرت تلك الصورة في ذاكرتي. لم أطلب يوما رؤية ألبوم حفلة عرس خالي، فطالما أن الأعراس موثقة عادة، ويجري التبليغ عنها من قبل المواطن والدولة، فأنا أستطيع ـعلى الأغلبـ الوصول إلى سجل الصور بسهولة.

المناسبة الثانية واضحة وتتضمن تفاصيل حيوية أكثر من سابقتها. وقد تكون المناسبة قد جرت في الوقت نفسه، لكنها لم توثق، وأنا لا أستطيع تحديد تاريخ حدوثها بشكل دقيق. أنا واثق من أنها جرت يوم السبت، لأنه

وحده القادر على صياغة الأجوبة. العمل يشير إليها أو إليك لا غير! فكرة أخرى، نحن باستمرار مشغولون بهويتنا، وربما ذلك ناجم عن العولمة، أو ربما لأننا كنا هكذا دائماً. هل لاحظت أنه منذ بدأت ثورة الإنترنت، هناك عدد أكبر من الأرشيفات التي تم إنشاؤها؟

وهل تظن أن ذلك يعود جزئياً إلى سعينا إلى الاحتفاظ بفرديتنا؟

قد يكون ذلك موضوع حوارنا القادم.

ما المحفز وراء عملك؟

الذاكرة.
شكراً على أسئلتك.

شكراً على أفكارك، دور، وشكراً أكثر على عملك.

ميترا عباس بور قيِّمة مساعدة في قسم التصوير الفوتوغرافي بمتحف الفن الحديث في نيويورك. وهي تترأس فريق بحث لدراسة التطور المادي والجمالي للتصوير الفوتوغرافي في أوائل القرن العشرين. وكان بحث الدكتوراه الذي قامت به قد ركز على أرشيفات الصور الفوتوغرافية وطرائق كتابتها لتاريخ التصوير الفوتوغرافي في الشرق الأوسط.

الأحد ثلاث ساعات بسبب ضرورة الترجمة، وهناك بالتأكيد أجزاء من الخطبة "تضيع في الترجمة". في فيلم الفيديو "40 يوماً" ترين القس يقرأ من ورقة محمولة أمام وجهه، كي يتذكر أسماء أفراد عائلة المتوفى. إنها المرة الأولى في الفيديو التي تشاهدين فيها وجهاً بشرياً، وهو قد أخفي في أغلب الوقت بتلك الورقة البيضاء، وكأنها غائب عن المكان.

تشكل العربية، واستعمال عاميتها اليومية، وسهولة امتزاجها بالعبرية الدارجة محلياً، خيطاً يتناسج عبر مسار الفيلم كله ابتداءً من تبادل التحية في المكالمات الهاتفية التي يبدأ الفيلم بها، وخلال كل أحاديث سميرة، إضافة إلى القداس الأخير الذي قرأه القس. ما هي أهمية العربية في سرد هذه القصة، في رسم بورتريه لجيل يعقوب وسميرة؟

هناك ثلاث لغات تلعب دوراً في فيديوهاتي؛ العربية اللغة الأم، التي تستعمل في فعل التذكر؛ والعبرية اللغة المكتسبة، التي تستعمل بشكل أساسي لوصف الأحداث التي تقع بعد الحرب؛ والإغريقية المستعملة في الممارسة الدينية، التي لا نفهمها إطلاقاً.

السرد القصصي لـ "40 يوماً" شعري. فبدلاً من التعريف بالشخصيات هناك عرض لملامحهم البارزة، ووصف سلسلة من الأحداث التي وقعت ضمن الفيلم، فأنت تقدم سلسلة من اللقطات المؤطرة بإحكام للإيماءات والتفاصيل والرموز.

أنت وصفته بشكل جميل. القصة تحكى بواسطة إيماءات الأيدي.

تعقيدات الهوية ـدينياً وثقافياً ولغوياً ومحلياً وتاريخياًـ موضوع مركزي على امتداد عملك. وهذا التعقيد غالباً ما يتم الكشف عنه من خلال وثائق جزئية أو أسئلة من دون إجابات. هل يمكنك التحدث عن دور المجهول في ممارستك؟

نعم. من الواضح أن هناك أسئلة أكثر في عملي من الأجوبة، فأنت تغادرين العمل وما زالت لديك العديد من الأسئلة التي تطرحينها على نفسك. إنها حالة رائعة للعقل عندما يُدفع لطرح الأسئلة. والفرد هو

عند ربطه بسكانوغرامات، التي تتناول فصولاً معقدة ومهمشة تماماً من التاريخ في شكل صور عائلية شخصية وصريحة؛ كيف يمكن لتفاصيل حيوات هؤلاء الأفراد أن تعبر عن هموم أكثر شمولية؟

ما يحدد طائفة ما كأقلية هي المبادئ التأسيسية لهذه الدولة، وهذا لا يعني أن الأقلية أقل عدداً من غيرها فقط، بل بإمكانك أن تجد الأقليات المحددة على أساس الجنس، والتعليم، والوضع الاقتصادي، ... وهلم جرا. ففي الحقيقة، نحن جميعاً، وفي لحظة ما من حياتنا، نستشعر تجربة أننا ننتمي إلى الأقلية، لكن لدى البعض منا يتم كبت هذه الحالة. يمكنك أن تطلعي على عملي وتقلصيه إلى تصريح جمالي يتعلق بثقافتي، أو تريه تاريخاً لمنطقتي، أو حتى نوعاً من فن سرد حكاية ما. وكل هذه التأويلات صحيحة. لكنني آمل أن يتمحور أيضاً حول التضامن الإنساني. فعبارة ''أقلية ضمن أقلية'' أصبحت نوعاً من المجاز في عملي، وبالنسبة لعينيّ نحن جميعاً فلسطينيون مسيحيون. فمقبرتك أنت أيضاً قد تتعرض للتدمير في يوم ما... .

يتباطأ الفيلم مرات عدة فوق شيء غائب تماماً. يحضرني مشهد حجر قبر عليه نصف صليب، والنقش على النصف المفقود الآخر مطلي بلون خلفية الحجر الباهت؛ أو في حفل التأبين (حفل ''الأربعين'') داخل الكنيسة، حيث غطت قطعة ورق بيضاء رأس القس؛ أو تلك الصورة المؤثرة؛ صورة القدم التي تتمدد فتخرج تحت ضوء الصباح من السرير، مهملةً رنين الهاتف. ما هو دور الغياب ـبصرياً ومفهومياًـ في معرض ''40 يوماً''؟

دور الغياب هو خلق فراغ لك كي تملئيه. وهو يعكس أيضاً عدم قدرتنا على نقل القصة بالكامل، سواء بصرياً أو مفهومياً. سأستطرد مع غائب واحد، يتطلب شرحاً: الورقة البيضاء المجعدة في الفيديو عند تصوير حفل التأبين الذي جرى بعد 40 يوماً. في التركيبات السابقة، تعاملت مع علاقة معقدة ما بين الطائفة المسيحية والكنيسة الأرثوذوكسية. فهناك فجوة ثقافية ما بين زعماء الكنيسة الذين هم من أوروبا، ورعايا الكنيسة العرب. في تركيبي الذي يحمل اسم ''كنيسة القديس جورجياوس'' (2009)، ترين القس يلقي خطبته باللغة الإغريقية، وهي لغة غير مفهومة لجمهور الكنيسة، بينما هناك مترجم من الطائفة يقوم بترجمة كلماته إلى العربية. يستغرق قداس

الفلسطينيين المسيحيين باعتباره أرشيفاً يستند إلى فحص ضوئي رقمي. إنها صورتها في نهاية المطاف، وهي بيدها لها الحق كمالكة أن تدمرها، أو أن تخفيها في مطبخها.

يقدم معرض "40 يوماً" أولا إحصائيات عن الفلسطينيين المسيحيين في اللد، وفي إسرائيل، إضافة إلى تقديم كشف عن التشويه المتكرر لمقبرة المسيحيين في المدينة. وعلى خلفية تلك الحقائق الموضوعية، تتكشف صورة بورتريه حميمة لزوجين. وتلك اللقطات التي أخذها يعقوب لتوثيق أعمال التشويه التي تلحق بالمقبرة وتفسير سميرة لها، كأنها صفحات من ألبوم عائلي، تربط ما بين السياسي والشخصي. متى علمتَ بصور المقبرة هذه؟ هل تحدثتَ مع يعقوب عنها؟ كيف تربط هذين النصفين من الفيلم بعضهما ببعض: موضوع مقبرة اللد وموضوع يعقوب وسميرة؟

لم يتكلم أيٌّ منا نحن الثلاثة: أنا ويعقوب وسميرة، حول الصور من قبل. فمع وجود الكاميرا باعتبارها عيننا الثالثة، كانت القصص تبدأ عندما تكون الكاميرا في طور الاستعمال. فهي تخلق مباشرة مجموعة من العلاقات ما بيننا، وهذه تربط القصتين في الفيديو، كما جاء في طرحك الدقيق. ومثل معظم أعمالي في حقل أفلام الفيديو، يقدم "40 يوماً" قصة شخصية للغاية أربطها بسرد قصصي أوسع. وفي هذه الحالة، تشكل وفاة يعقوب، وحفل التأبين الخاص به بعد 40 يوماً على رحيله، لحمة السرد القصصي، وفي الوقت نفسه قصة المكان الذي دفن فيه، مقبرة المسيحيين في اللد، التي تتعرض للتخريب المتعمد مرة كل بضع سنوات على يد مجاميع تنتمي إلى ديانات أخرى. إنها جريمة كراهية. ولعلها ليست سوى مسألة وقت قبل أن يتم تدمير قبره أيضاً. يمكن القول إن تدمير المقبرة يعكس وضع المسيحيين كأقلية، ويعكس، بشكل عام، الحال الإنساني حين لا يملك المرء حصانة تحميه.

يتحدد موقع الفيلم تاريخياً من خلال تكريسه ليعقوب منيِّر الذي عاش ما بين العامين 1920و2011، وضمن الإطار الزمني الذي وضعته سميرة وهي تتحدث عن نقوش القبور الخاصة بأفراد العائلة، وبخاصة أمها التي ماتت العام 1979 عن سن الثمانين. ومن هذا المنظور، يتمثل تاريخ كل القرن العشرين من خلال حياة كل شخصية من شخصيات الفيلم. أرى ذلك

تواريخ أخرى، تعود إلى الوقت الذي انفتحت فيه عدسة الكاميرا، ثم جرى طبع الصورة.

أفهم أفكارك جيداً، مع ذلك، يجب الاعتراف بأنني بصفتي قيِّمة صور فوتوغرافية، جفلتُ أثناء مشاهدتي معرض "40 يوماً" حين مزقت سميرة صوراً فوتوغرافية لمقبرة اللد وهي تردد متأوهة: "يجب القيام بذلك". في الوقت نفسه، أعجبتُ كثيراً بالقوة الرمزية التي تحملها هذه المبادرة، التي تشدد على مادية تلك الصور وهشاشتها ككيانات وسجلات تاريخية. ما هي علاقتك بتلك الصور الفوتوغرافية كدليل وكتاريخ؟ وكيف صاغت تلك الأفكار ممارستك الفنية عليها؟

بالتأكيد أشاركك الشعور نفسه بالتوتر، حين وقع ذلك الحادث، إذ أخذت نفساً عميقاً وأنا أراقبها تدمر الصور بشكل قاسٍ. كان بإمكاني أخذ الصور من يدها وفصلها بأناة عن الرطوبة التي جعلتها تلتصق بعضها ببعض، لكن فعل التمزيق ذاك كان حقاً من حقوقها. والآن، أصبح لدينا قصة تلك الصور ككيانات، ولغرض التمكن من سرد الحكاية بالكامل كان "يجب القيام بذلك". فقصتا تلك الصورة تتقاطعان هنا بطريقة شعرية: المحتوى البنيوي هو توثيق فعل التدمير، والطريقة الرهيبة التي جمعت هذه الصور معاً ثم انفصلت عن بعضها البعض، وتاريخ الصورة الفوتوغرافية ككيان هو طبقة ثانية من التدمير.

يقدم فيديو "40 يوماً" فرصة لمشاهدة عملية مُسرَّعة للتدخل في الصور الأصلية. فأنا جلست مع سميرة في غرفة الجلوس، وكانت الكاميرا بيننا، وبقينا نتكلم حول تدمير المقبرة المسيحية في مدينتنا. أخبرتني أن جدي، يعقوب، التقط صوراً ليوثق هذا الفعل العنيف ويقدم الدلائل عنه للشرطة، كإثبات رسمي. كان ذلك هو التوثيق الوحيد لعملية هدم المقبرة، ولأن الشرطة لم تحل القضية، استرجع الصور منها. وقد أبقتها سميرة في جرار بالمطبخ، وهناك تعرضت للرطوبة المتأتية من الطبخ، وهي قد أرسلتني للمطبخ لأخذها حين كنا نصور. وعادة، تعكس سكانوغراماتي سنوات من الانحلال، لكن في هذه الحالة كانت قصة الشيء-الصورة قد اكتملت في غضون دقائق، خلال قيامي بالتصوير. هذا الفيديو يحافظ على المنطق نفسه لمشروع أرشيف

إليه ''السكانوغرامات'' هو جلب هذه القصة إلى السطح.

وأنت تصف هذه العملية، أجد نفسي مذهولة أمام حقيقة كونك حالَمَا تحوّل الصور الفوتوغرافية إلى سكانوغرامات، يصبح لكل صورة مؤلفان وتاريخا تكوين مختلفان: ذلك الخاص بالصورة الأصلية، ثم إعادة إحيائك لها بشكل وسياق جديدين. كيف لثنائية التاريخ والتأليف أن تكشف نفسها في السكانوغرامات؟

السكانوغرامات، تحكي قصتين (بتاريخين مختلفين) يكمل أحدهما الآخر: الأولى هي ذات محتوى بنيوي للصورة. فعلى سبيل المثال: ''سميرة في ثوب عرسها''. أما الأخرى فهي قصة الصورة الفوتوغرافية نفسها منذ أنُطبعت: الحُفر والطيات وأيضاً كون صور عرس سميرة قد حفِظت تحت السرير ولم يتم تنظيمها والحفاظ عليها ''بشكل مناسب'' في ألبوم. أما سكانوغرام صورة العرس الفوتوغرافية، فيخبرنا بتاريخ ما يرفضون التحدث عنه مباشرة. إنه ذلك التاريخ الذي ظل قائماً بشكل لاشعوري فقط، على الرغم من وجوده مادياً عبر الصور الفوتوغرافية.

هل ترى عملك باعتباره تفاعلاً مع مصور أصلي؟

نعم. لكن ليس من خلال جهاز المسح الضوئي الخاص بي، بل من خلال التخلي الذي قمتُ به عن الصور الأصلية، فأنا غالباً لا أحتفظ بالصور الفوتوغرافية الأصلية. أنا بعد إجراء المسح الضوئي للصورة، أو أي وثيقة أخرى، أقوم بإعادتها لأصحابها. هدف أرشيف الفلسطينيين المسيحيين في الشتات هو أن يصبح قاعدة بيانات على الإنترنت، وأنا غير مهتم بانتزاع الصورة الفوتوغرافية من مكانها الأصلي في ''الأكياس البلاستيكية''. وقد تختفي المواد مع مرور الوقت في يِد أصحابها. وهذه هي قصة الصورة الفوتوغرافية، فهي تملك عمراً محدداً إذا لم تقومي بحفظها في شروط أرشيفية. أعرف أنه أمر صعب أن يسمح شخص معني جداً في البحث في الأرشيفات للمواد الأصلية أن تفلت من يده، لكن هذه هي طبيعة هذا الشكل الفني الذي نسميه بـ ''التصوير الفوتوغرافي''، وأنا أحترمه. لذلك، فإن السكانوغرام هو نقطة واحدة في زمن وتاريخ محددين، ويتفاعل مع

مشروع الأرشيف الفلسطيني المسيحي الذي يعد الوحيد، اليوم، المكرس للشتات الفلسطيني- المسيحي. لقد كان هذا الأرشيف نقطة تحول في ممارستي الفنية، وهو يقدم الأساس لكل تركيباتي القابلة لأن تكون صورة فوتوغرافية واحدة، أو سلسلة من 15 صورة تُطرح وكأنها ألبوم عائلي. أدركتُ، حين بدأت الكتابة والتسجيل والتصوير (كجزء من محاولتي لجعل المواد متناصّة)، لماذا جمعت جدتي كل تلك الصور ووضعتها تحت جانب السرير الذي ينام جدي عليه، وكأنها حضور في اللاوعي اللاشعوري، لكنها تجسيد مادي أيضاً. وهذا يعود لأنه لا يمكن وضع هذه الصور ضمن صنف ''الألبومات العائلية''؛ فهي دليل على حياة ''ما قبل'' و''ما بعد'' (وبعضها حتى خلال) عام واحد (1948) من نكبة متواصلة.

نوعية المادة التي تشكلت الصورة الفوتوغرافية الأصلية منها، من حيث نسيج سطحها وتجعداته وحفره، ومن حيث الدلائل على معالجتها، قد سلط الضوء عليها بما أطلقتَ عليه اسم ''سكانوغرام''. هل من الممكن أن توضح أهمية التشديد على أن الصورة الفوتوغرافية التاريخية ليست صورة فحسب، بل هي كيان أيضاً؟

أتفق مع وصفك. فمعنى ''سكانوغرام'' هو بالضبط الرسم بجهاز المسح الضوئي. فكل ''سكانوغرام'' معمول من ثلاث طبقات من المسح الضوئي، وكل مسح مبرمَج لكشف جانب مختلف من المادة. بعد ذلك، قمتُ بوضع الطبقات في صورة واحدة. فـ''السكانوغرام'' هو تأويلي الشخصي لمادة تاريخية مأخوذة من الأرشيف الفلسطيني المسيحي. ومن الطبيعي أن تعتمد العملية على الجانب الشخصي، وتكون النتيجة مختلفة عن الصورة الأصلية. يمكن القول إن تقنية المسح الصوري المتعدد، تشدد على تاريخ الوثيقة باعتبارها كياناً ملموساً، وهذا يعني أن الشقوق والحفر تصبح ذات أهمية كبيرة وتقريباً تأخذ، بطريقة مجردة، ثلاثة أبعاد في حجمها وقياساتها. وتعرض الـ ''سكانوغرامات'' طرائق في إعادة تقديم هذه الوثائق ورؤيتها من خلال صور مطبوعة ذات درجة عالية وحادة من الوضوح. ويجري عادة تفعيل ''السكانوغرامات'' باعتبارها ''كيانات'' معاصرة، أو كي أكون أكثر دقة، نتيجة لوضعها المادي المعاصر. بصيغة أخرى، الصورة الفوتوغرافية هي كيان مادي، له تاريخ قائم بذاته، وما تسعى

ميترا عباس بور تحاور دور غويز
الصور هي بمثابة لاوعي مجسم وملموس

لنبدأ من البداية، متى وضمن أي سياق بدأتَ تعمل على صور فوتوغرافية تاريخية؟

بدأتُ أعمل على الأرشيفات العام 2006، كجزء من دراستي وبحثي لأطروحة الدكتوراه عن التصوير الفوتوغرافي ذي الطابع الاستشراقي في الأرشيفات الصهيونية. وبعد ثلاث سنوات بدأت العمل على لقطات أرشيفية بصفتي فناناً بصرياً لا كاتباً فقط.

في العام 2009، وجدتُ حقيبة ملابس موضوعة تحت سرير جدّيّ، محشوة بأكياس بلاستيكية مملوءة بصور فوتوغرافية ووثائق أخرى تعود إلى النصف الأول من القرن العشرين. لم أكن قد رأيت من قبل تلك المواد، وأذكر أنني تساءلت لماذا لم يتم تنظيمها في ألبومات عائلية مثلما يحفظ الناس، عادة، ذلك النوع من الصور الخاصة بالأعراس، والتعميد، وصور الأستديوهات، وأعياد الميلاد، وغير ذلك. وبعد الاستئذان من جدَّيَ، توليتُ مهمة تنظيمها في ألبومات. حاولت في تلك المهمة ترتيب القصص التقليدية التي تحملها الألبومات العائلية في طياتها من خلال ترتيب الصور نفسها. وبصفتي المؤرخ غير الرسمي للعائلة، وربما كوني أكبر الأحفاد، سمح لي جدَّايَ بالتعامل مع هذه المواد. وهكذا وجدت نفسي أحرر تواريخنا مرة بعد أخرى بنسخ وإمكانيات مختلفة، لكنني فشلت في المهمة الأولية التي أخذتها على عاتقي، والمتمثلة في عمل ألبومات عائلية. أدركتُ ـآنذاكـ ما كانت جدتي تعيه طوال الوقت: إنها مهمة مستحيلة. فهي قد أعطتني وقتاً للوصول إلى ذلك الاستنتاج وحدي، مثلما كان الحال معها في الماضي.

هل من الممكن التحدث عن أهمية العمل على مادة تاريخية بالنسبة إليك؟

هذا العثور المحكوم بالمصادفة لحقيبة واحدة، كان نقطة انطلاق

المنفى في عمان ـ الأردن. لذلك، فإن معرض غويز يحمل بين طياته مفارقة ـأن يقوم بتنظيم المعرض هنا في لندن سليلان لُدِيّيْن، أحدهما إسرائيلي فلسطيني، والآخر فلسطيني بريطاني، يقومان بإعادة تأكيد مشترك للوجود الفلسطيني في اللد، في عاصمة إمبراطورية عجوز، تتحمل الكثير من مسؤولية انهيار الشام المتسامح والمنفتح، وفتح المجال لتأسيس دولة إسرائيل، وما زالت على الرغم من ذلك، تتدخل، في الفترة الأخيرة، في شؤون المنطقة بشكل كارثي.

لندن، ربيع 2013

---

[1] اشتهرت مدينة اللد بأنها مسقط رأس والدة القديس جرجس أو الخضر كما تعرفه الثقافة الشعبية المشتركة لدى الأديان كلها في فلسطين . انه أيضاً القديس الراعي لانجلترا! الا أن مدينة اللد فقدت معظم آثارها العربية المسيحية والاسلامية وأصبحت اليوم معروفة كعاصمة المخدرات في اسرائيل ومن أكثر مدنها فقراً وعنفاً.

[2] انظر إلى الحوار ما بين دور غويز وميترا عباس بور، ص: 70.

عمر القطان سينمائي وأمين سر مجلس أمناء مؤسسة عبد المحسن القطان ويدير حالياً البرنامج الفني لقاعات الموزاييك

مسلمين أم مسيحيين أم يهوداً، متوافقين مع بعضهم البعض (وطبعاً كان من النادر أن يأتي ذكر الملحدين ضمن هذا السياق)!

وبتلك الروح، أُمرنا بعدم التمييز ما بين الناس على أساس دياناتهم. مع ذلك، هل كان والدانا مثاليين بل وربما ساذجين، لتقليلهم عمق الموالاة الطائفية لدى الإنسان العربي، والمدى الذي ظلت مجتمعاتنا وفقه مقيدة بالنظام العثماني القائم على سيادة حكم الأغلبية، مقابل حكم ذاتي محدود للأقلية؟ ما هو أكيد أن هذا النظام ما عاد قابلاً للاستمرار في فترة ما بعد الحرب العالمية الأولى.

وضمن هذا السياق، نأمل أن تروا في هذا المعرض الغني والمثير للمشاعر، أن عمل غويز هو إعادة تأكيد لإمكانيات مختلفة لمدينته، وللمنطقة بشكل أوسع. فهو يقدم تحدياً جريئاً أمام محاولة المسح التاريخي لواقع مصرٍّ على الاستمرار، ضمن ديناميكية معاصرة لا تكف عن إنكاره وتدميره في آن واحد، وبشكل عنيف ولاعقلاني. لذلك، فإن هذا الإصرار الفني، على هشاشته وفعله الأرشيفي وبعده التراجيدي، يكشف أيضاً عن أنه حاضر على الرغم من محاولة تغييبه، ومتشبث بالحياة ولن يغادر!

يشير عنوان معرض غويز: ''40 يوماً''، إلى فترة انتهاء الحداد؛ إنه الفاصل القائم ما بين العزاء والبدء من جديد. يضم مشروع غويز أرشيفاً فلسطينياً ـ مسيحياً،[2] لكن هذا الأرشيف بُعثت فيه الحياة على يد سليل حي، حتى لو كانت هويته قد أعاد التاريخ صياغتها. لكن أيّاً منا يستطيع الزعم بامتلاك هوية ثابتة لا تتغير؟

لقد ولدت جدتي (أم والدي) في اللّد، وكانت المدينة آخر ملاذ لجأت إليه عائلة والدي خلال نزوحهم من فلسطين في صيف العام 1948، على طريق طويل نحو

يجدون أنفسهم رهائن ظلم وتدمير يفوقان الوصف. إنه حال مأساوي تشترك فيه العديد من مناطق العالم اليوم.

هذا الواقع كان أحد الأسباب التي جعلتنا ندعو دور غويز لعرض عمله في قاعات الموزاييك. فمن المفارقة، أن دور غويز كان نتاجاً لاختلاط نادر جمع ما بين مناسبتين تاريخيتين متعارضتين: طرد معظم الفلسطينيين من وطنهم العام 1948، وما أعقبه من إنشاء دولة إسرائيل، التي هو الآن مواطن فيها. فأم غويز من اللد، وهي ابنة إحدى العائلات الفلسطينية التي بقيت في المدينة بعد إخراج أغلب سكانها البالغ عددهم حوالي 20 ألف شخص آنذاك، ولم يسمح لهم بالعودة بعد انتهاء حرب العام 1948. كذلك، لغويز جانب يهودي تونسي ورثه عن أبيه، الذي كان واحداً من المهاجرين إلى دولة إسرائيل الجديدة خلال عقد الخمسينيات من القرن العشرين، وإلى اللد[1] التي أطلق الاحتلال عليها لاحقاً اسم ”لود“.

لذلك، فإنه ليس غريباً أن يكون عمله معنياً بديناميكيات العلاقات ما بين الأغلبية والأقلية، فمع اختفاء ثقافات الأقليات في بلادنا، هناك بالمقابل جهود شخصية بطولية تسعى إلى إبقاء ذكراهم حية. لكن هذا العمل يدعونا، أيضاً، إلى التساؤل عما تعنيه الوطنية والإثنية، ويحثنا على التفكير في عملية كتابة التاريخ، كما يشرح الفنان لاحقاً في هذا الكتاب، خلال مقابلته مع ميترا عباس بور.

خلال نشأتي في بيروت في سبعينيات القرن الماضي، لم يكن يسمح لي بالاستفسار عن دين الآخر، على الرغم من أنه كان من الصعب عدم الانتباه للانقسامات الطائفية حولنا (أو في الحقيقة إلى تلك الرموز الدينية التي كان وما زال يرتديها الكثيرون من الناس). فوالداي، مثل الكثير من القوميين العلمانيين من ذلك الوقت، كانا يحلمان بمجتمع متحرر من تلك الانقسامات، وبقيا يشيران إلى ماض ـلكن إلى أي ماض؟ـ كان الكل فيه، سواء أكانوا

مقدمة
عمر القطان

"احذر من أن تقول لهم إن مدناً مختلفة تتبع، أحياناً، إحداها الأخرى، في الموقع نفسه، وتحت الاسم نفسه، تولد وتموت من دون أن تعرف إحداها الأخرى، ومن دون أن تتواصل في ما بينها. وفي بعض الأحيان، تبقى أسماء الساكنين كما هي، وكذلك لهجاتهم، بل وملامح وجوههم. لكن الآلهة التي تعيش تحت أسماء محددة، وفوق أماكن محددة، تكون قد رحلت من دون أي كلمة، وجاء أغراب استوطنوا مكانها" (ايتالو كالفينو، مدن غير مرئية، ص: 31—30.).

إنه لأمر يبعث على الأسى أن ينظَّم أول معرض منفرد لدور غويز في قاعات الموزاييك بلندن، في الوقت الذي يشهد فيه العالم العربي حرباً أهلية ضارية وعنفاً طائفياً لا متناهي، فنحن الذين كنا محظوظين بالنشوء في مدن مختلطة من تلك المنطقة ـبيروت، ودمشق، وبغداد، والقاهرةـ رحنا نرى تلك الأنسجة المدينية الغنية بألوانها ونقوشها تتفكك. وكأن نسيج منطقتنا، على الرغم من غناه وقدمه وغزارة ألوانه، لم يكن قادراً على مواجهة الحداثة، سواء أخذت هذه الحداثة شكل الصهيونية ومشروعها الإثني—الاستعماري، أو شكل شكلها القومي العربي العلماني بمختلف مظاهره، أو، شكلها الأخير؛ المتمثل بالحركات الإسلامية بكل أطيافها القومية. واليوم، نشاهد بلداناً عربية عدة وهي تنزف أمام أعيننا: فالعراق فقد أغلب أقلياته للهجرة، ولعل سوريا سائرة على الطريق نفسه، ولبنان قنبلة طائفية موقوتة، بينما يعيش الفلسطينيون؛ سواء في إسرائيل، أو الذين يعيشون في مناطق السلطة الفلسطينية، ظروفاً أكثر تهميشاً من ذي قبل، وما زالوا يرزحون تحت تهديد متزايد بالتهجير، في حين يعيش أقباط مصر حالة عميقة من القلق وانعدام الأمن. وليست هناك حاجة للقول إن المواطنين من جميع الإثنيات والطوائف، وبخاصة الفقراء والمحرومين،

يهدف برنامجنا إلى استكشاف محطات هذا الفشل وعواقبه الإنسانية والسياسية والاجتماعية عبر الفن، والعمارة، والأدب، والموسيقى، والسينما. فبعيداً عن أن يكون مجرد مشروع أكاديمي حنيني، فإنه يطمح لكشف تلك العمليات التي آلت إلى هذا الفشل. وفي الوقت نفسه، سيعمل على استكشاف آلية استمرار سكان هذه المدن في مقاومة تفكك بيئاتهم أو دمارها من خلال مشاريع مدنية، أو من خلال التعبير الفني، أو من خلال قصص العشاق لا غير!

هذا مشروع طموح وطويل الأمد، سيتمحور أولاً حول عدد من المناسبات التي ستنظم على مدار عام كامل في قاعات الموزاييك بلندن، ابتداءً من ربيع العام 2013 مع معرض دور غويز: 40 يوماً. كذلك، نسعى إلى إجراء جولة في منطقة الشرق الأوسط، وعلى المستوى العالمي، لبعض هذه النشاطات، إضافة إلى توثيق البرنامج في إصدارات متنوعة.

شكر وتقدير

تقدم قاعات الموزاييك خالص شكرها لأرييلا ازولي لمساهمتها في تحقيق هذا المعرض، إضافة إلى هايدي زوكرمان جيكوبسون مديرة متحف أسبن التي اختارت درو غويز للإقامة الدولية التابعة لآرت سبيس في سان أنتونيو، ولجاليري آرت سبيس ـ سان أنتونيو للتعاون في إنتاج "40 يوماً".

حول ”مدن عربية في طور الاختفاء“

”مدن عربية في طور الاختفاء“ برنامج ثقافي طموح يسلط الضوء على دمار الحياة المدينية في العالم العربي في عصر ما بعد الاستعمار، يتضمن عدداً من المعارض والمحاضرات والأفلام على امتداد أعوام عدة.

المدينة هي فضاء تصبح الحياة المدنية فيه ممكنة، ويصبح ذوبان الانقسامات القبلية والإثنية والطائفية للسكان الذين استقروا فيه ممكناً أيضاً، لتتحول إلى أشكال اجتماعية غير مألوفة محكومة بقواعد وقوانين جديدة. كذلك، فالمدن مراكز لمقاومة الغازي والتمرد على الظلم. وفيها يلتقي العشاق أيضاً من دون فيها اعتبار لخلفياتهم، ويكتشفون فضاءات جديدة في المخيلة لم يكن ممكناً التفكير فيها قط في الريف، أو الصحراء، يطورون أنواعاً جديدة من العلاقات. والمدينة تصوغ مدارك طفولتنا، وعلاقتنا مع الضوء والصوت، ومع الفضاء والمنظور.

ومع ذلك، فإن المدن لا تتردد في خيانة سكانها، ففيها خفايا الحشرات والقوارض، وفيها القذارة والتلوث، إضافة إلى مسارح الفوضى، والحروب الأهلية والمذابح. ففي العالم العربي الحديث، كانت المدن مخادعة وغدّارة، إذ أنها منحت المواطن وعوداً بسيادة القانون، والسلم الاجتماعي، والمساواة، والحرية، لتتحول إلى سجون وشراك له، فغالباً ما يُطرد منها، أو يتعرض فيها للاضطهاد بسبب لغته أو دينه (أو لعدم إيمانه أصلاً!).

شهدت، وبدرجات مختلفة، مدن مثل يافا، وبيروت، واللد، وبغداد، والقاهرة، وحلب، والبصرة، وطرابلس (لبنان وليبيا)، ومدينة الكويت، والقدس، ومقديشو، دماراً وعنفاً رهيبين خلال عصر ما بعد الاستعمار، وهذا ما يمكن وصفه بأنه فشل للمشروع المديني.

المحتويات

فريق قاعات الموزاييك:
رئيسة البرمجة والعمليات: ريتشل هورنزبي
مشرفة المعرض: أنجلينا رديكوفيتش
التسويق والصحافة: دانيال لوكاس

الصور بإذن من جاليري دفير وكارليه جيباور.
الترجمة إلى العربية: لؤي عبد الإله وعمر القطان
تدقيق لغة عربية: عبد الرحمن أبو شمّالة
تدقيق لغة إنجليزية: سوزان ماجوير
تصميم الكتالوج: هايبركت

تم نشر هذا الدليل بمناسبة معرض 40 يوماً لدور غويز الذي أقيم في
قاعات الموزايك في لندن من 12 نيسان حتى 31 أيار 2013
www.mosaicrooms.org

بدعم من مؤسسة عبد المحسن القطان

ISBN 978-9950-313-42-2

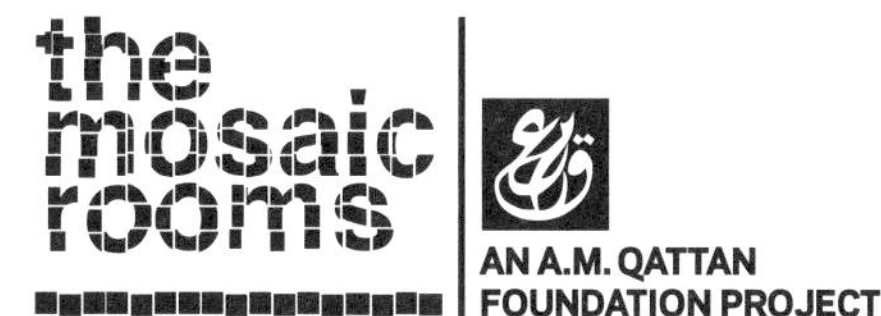

دور غويز

40 يوماً